DOUGLAS REEVES

ELEMENTS of GRADING

SECOND EDITION

A Guide to Effective Practice

Solution Tree | Press

a division of
Solution Tree

555 North Morton Street
Bloomington, IN 47404
800.733.6786 (toll free) / 812.336.7700
FAX: 812.336.7790

email: info@solution-tree.com
solution-tree.com

Visit go.solution-tree.com/assessment to download the reproducibles in this book.

Printed in the United States of America

19   18   17   16   15   1   2   3   4   5

Library of Congress Cataloging-in-Publication Data

Reeves, Douglas B., 1953- author.

  Elements of grading : a guide to effective practice / Douglas Reeves. -- Second edition.

       pages cm

  Includes bibliographical references and index.

  ISBN 978-1-936763-89-4 (perfect bound) 1. Grading and marking (Students)--Handbooks, manuals, etc. I. Title.

  LB3051.R3554 2016

  371.27'2--dc23

                              2015029666

Solution Tree
Jeffrey C. Jones, CEO
Edmund M. Ackerman, President

Solution Tree Press
President: Douglas M. Rife
Senior Acquisitions Editor: Amy Rubenstein
Editorial Director: Lesley Bolton
Managing Production Editor: Caroline Weiss
Senior Production Editor: Christine Hood
Copy Editors: Sarah Payne-Mills & Miranda Addonizio
Text and Cover Designer: Abigail Bowen

Mary, to whom this book is dedicated,
cares much more about family, friends, and
animals than she ever will about grades.
May it always be so.

ACKNOWLEDGMENTS

I am particularly indebted to leading scholars in this field, including Thomas Guskey, Lee Ann Jung, Bob Marzano, Ken O'Connor, Rick DuFour, and Rick Wormeli.

In addition, the prolific contributors to standards-based learning, teaching, and grading at #SBLChat consistently challenge my thinking on this subject.

Those at Solution Tree, including publisher Douglas Rife, CEO Jeff Jones, president Ed Ackerman, and senior production editor Christine Hood, make every project far better than my original manuscript. If I am the foundation of this town meeting house, then they are surely the walls, roof, and steeple.

—Douglas Reeves

Visit **go.solution-tree.com/assessment** to download
the reproducibles in this book.

TABLE OF CONTENTS

Chapter 12

Grading for Students With Special Needs 139

Chapter 13

The Impact of Technology on Grading Practices . . . 145

Conclusion

Inspiring Change in Grading Policies. 153

ABOUT THE AUTHOR

 **Douglas Reeves, PhD,** is the author of more than thirty books and eighty articles about education, leadership, and organizational effectiveness. He has presented his work on effective grading practices to audiences around the world. His research appears in *Educational Leadership*, *Kappan*, *The American School Board Journal*, and many other publications. His comments on grading appeared on the cover of *USA Today*, and his work remains frequently cited in professional and academic publications. Douglas's honors include the Distinguished Service Award from the National Association of Secondary School Principals, the Brock International Prize, and the Contribution to the Field Award from the National Staff Development Council (now Learning Forward). He is the founding editor and copublisher of *The SNAFU Review*, where he provides one-on-one support for disabled veterans whose writing and art inspire others with post-traumatic stress disorder. He is also the founder of Finish the Dissertation, a free and noncommercial service for doctoral students. He lives with his family in downtown Boston.

To learn more about Douglas's work, visit Creative Leadership Solutions (CreativeLeadership.net) or the Change Leaders blog (www.changeleaders.com), or follow him on Twitter @DouglasReeves.

To book Douglas Reeves for professional development, contact pd@solution-tree.com.

FINDING COMMON GROUND

Standards-based grading is one of the most controversial issues in 21st century education. The two sides in the debate can be contentious, even rancorous, challenging one another's motives and concern for students. This book is not designed to tell the critics of standards-based grading that they are wrong. Rather, I attempt to seek common ground between the critics and advocates of standards-based grading to develop and promote the most effective grading practices.

So let's step back from the brink and attempt a more rational dialogue with the critics of standards-based grading. I'm not one to back away from a vigorous debate on important issues, but this particular debate has gone off the rails from policy disagreements to destructive monologues. We can do better. Although standards-based grading is the logical accompaniment to any system that uses standards, there remains a wide gulf between the embrace of standards and the use of standards-based grading. The policy of standards-based grading is the reality in only a small fraction of districts. Although the practice is growing, the opposition is consistent and strong. What is missing in the debate between advocates and critics is a thoughtful dialogue about the strengths and weaknesses of standards-based grading.

To begin, let's try to find some common ground. Before making the case for standards-based grading and explaining why it's such a great idea, we should acknowledge the legitimate concerns that the critics—particularly parents—have about changes in grading practices that affect their children. For example, you might begin the conversation by asking the following five questions.

1. Can we all agree that grades should be fair? Two students with the same performance receive the same grade.

2. Can we all agree that grades should be accurate? The grade reflects the actual performance of the student.

3. Can we all agree that grades should be specific? Students and parents know exactly what is required for students to improve.

4. Can we all agree that grades should be timely? Students and parents receive information on student performance in sufficient time to make improvements.

5. Can we all agree that work ethic and personal responsibility are good ideas, even if we disagree about how to best achieve those goals? Some might believe that grading as a punishment system is effective, and others might believe that students respond best to constructive feedback.

Before turning another page of this book, engage in a brief conversation with a colleague who might be a skeptic about improvements in grading policy, and ask if you could find common ground on these five ideas. If so, you will have a much better opportunity to use this book as a vehicle for positive change in your school.

Skeptics and Cynics

I should distinguish between skeptics—resisters who demand evidence before accepting change—and cynics, for whom no amount of evidence is ever acceptable (Reeves, 2011b). In discussions of grading policies, skeptics often have sound reasons to doubt the claims of education reformers. The skeptics have seen one program after another accompanied by dubious research claims that show new ideas work miracles, only to find that the research was little more than a claim from a podium. Skeptics are the Galileos of education reform, demanding that evidence trump assertion, even when assertions are backed with authority. When it comes to grading policies, skeptics are asking the most reasonable of questions. Guskey (2002) suggests, "How's my kid doing?"

Similarly, teachers who believe deeply in their responsibility to shape students into people of character and responsibility know well that the student who derives pleasure only from instant gratification is not their customer. Instead, it is the student who must learn to accept difficult feedback and appreciate the value of deferred gratification. If grading-reform advocates would begin with the premise that those who challenge their positions are skeptics—teachers who care about their profession and parents who care about their children—then they have a much better chance to engage in dialogue characterized by reason and respect rather than anger and defensiveness.

Not every opponent of grading reform is a skeptic, earnestly searching for evidence and reasonably challenging suggested changes to present practices. Some of them are cynics. The cynics and skeptics appear quite similar in their questioning of new practices, but the stark differences quickly emerge. Skeptics consider the evidence, while cynics ignore it. Skeptics listen to the other side, while cynics only seek to hear themselves and an echo chamber of like-minded people. While the skeptics demand research, the cynics find no evidence sufficient to change present practices. Skeptics look at the evidence in a nuanced manner, realizing that no research is perfect and no reform carries a 100 percent guarantee, while cynics leap on any flaw to reject an entire proposal of improved grading practices.

A New Conversation About Grading

It's time for a new conversation about grading. If teachers, administrators, and researchers have learned anything from the controversies about grading, it is that evidence is not sufficient to sway public opinion on this emotional issue. Some of the most thoughtful scholars on this subject (Brookhart, 2003; Guskey, 2015; Hattie & Yates, 2014; Marzano, 2010; O'Connor, 2011; to name a few) provide a mountain of evidence, synthesized as follows.

- Feedback can be one of the most powerful influences on student achievement, provided it is fair, accurate, specific, and timely.

- Grading and test scores are the types of feedback that parents and policymakers most notice.

- Feedback that most influences student achievement is neither grades nor test scores but rather the minute-to-minute communication from teachers, peers, and students themselves.

- Toxic grading practices, such as the use of a 0 on a one hundred–point scale or the average to calculate final grades, have a demonstrably negative impact on the academic and behavioral performance of students.

- Effective grading practices—the subject of this book—provide a path to improved student results in engagement, attendance, behavior, and performance.

Taking these aspects into account, the second edition of *Elements of Grading* contains a significant amount of new content, including chapters on what the Common Core State Standards (CCSS) mean for grading practices and the impact of technology on grading systems. Thanks to the suggestions of many readers of the first edition, I have adopted the acronym FAST for the essential elements of grading—fair, accurate, specific, and timely.

If the benefits of effective grading practices and the negative consequences of toxic grading practices are so obvious, why is another book on the subject necessary? It's necessary because evidence is not sufficient when emotions and personal histories govern debates. Educators, parents, students, and administrators must have a conversation about the grading conversation. Parents and teachers who are firmly attached to grading practices of the 20th century are not co-conspirators against the best interests of students. Their personal experiences with grading systems from their own school days and scorn for dozens of failed education initiatives influence their views, all of which claim to be based on research and evidence.

When we approach these parents and teachers with changes in grading policies that represent a dramatic shift in both teacher practices and measures for student success, they are less apt to say, "Thank you" and more likely to say, "Wait a minute. This isn't the first time I've seen somebody suggest that we give students a break, and all it leads to is a breakdown in discipline and work ethic. All the talk about 'fewer failures' sounds suspiciously like 'everybody gets a trophy.' And from what I've seen, it's not working for students in my school or anywhere else." It is at this point that frustrated administrators demand buy-in, frustrated teachers take their dissent from the faculty meeting to the parking lot, and frustrated parents start marching to the next school board meeting. If we are to have a constructive conversation about grading practices, then a good start is to back off from the student points of view that dominate this debate and do something I have rarely seen: assume goodwill.

This book may not persuade the cynics, but my hope is that it engages the skeptics. If you are using this as part of a book study with faculty and parents, consider inviting participants to express their doubts and fears and share their personal experiences with reforms that failed. For the advocates of reform, my advice is to be less strident in claiming, "This will work!" and say instead, "Here is a hypothesis about the effects of improved grading policies—could we test that hypothesis, and see if it works with our students?"

As always, I welcome a continuing dialogue with readers, including those who disagree with the ideas presented in these pages.

Introduction

STARTING THE CONVERSATION

Whether you are a teacher or an administrator, parent or student, or policymaker or academic researcher, there are four essential questions to answer on the subject of grading. As previously emphasized, the elements of grading should be FAST—fair, accurate, specific, and timely.

- How can we make grading systems fair? What we describe as proficient performance truly must be a function of performance and not gender, ethnicity, or socioeconomic status.

- How can we make grading systems accurate? What we ascribe to students must be a matter of judgment as well as the consequence of evidence and reason.

- How can we make grading systems specific? Telling a student he or she is "average" or a "C" does little to help students, parents, and teachers collaborate for improved learning. Students must receive detailed information about their performance so they can use the feedback to improve.

- How can we make grading systems timely? Even if grades are fair, accurate, and specific, students cannot use feedback to improve performance unless the grades are provided in a timely manner.

In this book, we consider grading practices that meet all of these criteria and discuss practical ways for teachers to save time while providing effective feedback for students.

Fairness, accuracy, specificity, and timeliness—these elements are at the heart of any grading discussion. This book not only considers how to answer these four questions but also how to conduct constructive discussions about grading policies. Perfection is impossible in grading, and therefore, our quest is not for an ultimate answer. The goal is not perfect fairness but a system less subject to bias, both unintentional and deliberate; not perfect accuracy but a more accurate system; not absolute specificity but a system that provides feedback to help students know what they must do to improve. Finally, while it's not essential for feedback to always be immediate, the prevailing practice in which grades are delivered to students far too late for them to respond is unproductive. Many teachers work very hard to give students detailed feedback, but when that feedback is provided several weeks after student performance or, worst of all, after the semester has ended, then teachers have wasted their time.

As a teacher, I hope that the ways in which I give feedback are better forty years after I taught my first class than it was after thirty, but experience has taught me that the only certainty is that I will fall short of perfection. Therefore, I do not offer a simple recipe that readers can adopt with the confidence of certain success. Instead, these pages offer information regarding:

- A collegial process for discussing some of the most contentious issues in grading

- A communicative process for bringing all stakeholders—parents, board members, the media, students, union leaders, and policymakers—into the discussion

The importance of good communication about grading policies cannot be overstated. It is not sufficient to be right—that is, to have research, logic, and moral certainty on our side of an argument. If our ultimate goal is to make grading systems more effective (improve their fairness, accuracy, specificity, and timeliness), then we must be right on the merits of an argument and successful in reasoning with people who have different points of view.

Understanding Why Grading Is So Important

For teachers and school administrators, the feedback on student performance that perhaps gains the most attention is the annual exam. In Australia, the United Kingdom, and China, national tests are the coin of the realm, the assessments that mark students, teachers, schools, and entire education systems as successes or failures. In Canada, provincial examination scores assess students, schools, administrators, and teachers. Similarly, in the United States, the Elementary and Secondary Education Act (ESEA) of 1965 requires that each state tests students annually, although the nature and timing of those tests are decisions left to the states (Steinhauer & Rich, 2015).

Despite the political emphasis on annual tests, however, students and parents have a distinctly different focus than school personnel. Their attention is on classroom grades, report cards, and honor rolls. The question parents ask most often is not "What was your score on the exam?" but "How did you get that grade?" Moreover, grades determine academic honors and class rank, and they have a direct impact on college admissions and scholarship opportunities.

A 2008 Fairfax County Public Schools study indicates that 89 percent of colleges responding to a survey use grades to compare applicants, 39 percent require a minimum grade point average (GPA) for admissions into honors programs, and 33 percent require a minimum GPA for merit scholarships. More than half of the colleges do not recalculate grades based on the rigor or content of the course (Fairfax County Public Schools, Department of Accountability, 2008). Therefore, the grades that teachers assign can have a profound impact on students' future opportunities. The grades that students earn in middle school often influence their eligibility for college-preparatory coursework in high school. Similarly, decisions about which students qualify for advanced courses in middle school are influenced by the grades elementary school teachers assign. Grades also are important for both emotional and financial reasons; therefore, it is completely understandable that the topic of grading is sometimes fraught with contention.

Thomas Guskey and Jane Bailey (2001) document the century-long history of grading controversies. In just one system—Fairfax County, Virginia—there have been more than half a dozen different grading policies since 1912, with a variety of descriptive, numerical, and letter grading schemes. If we take into account the different systems in use at different schools, then the variation is even greater. The "standard" one hundred–point scale with ten-point intervals (90–100 = A; 80–89 = B; 70–79 = C; 60–69 = D; lower than 60 = F) dates from the 1960s, and it is now the most widely used system in the United States, according to high schools and colleges responding to the Fairfax survey (Fairfax County Public Schools, Department of Accountability, 2008).

Identifying What Influences Grades

Most teachers, parents, and school administrators assume that the biggest influence on grades is the individual student's performance. At first glance, such an assumption seems reasonable, but as you will learn in the following pages, a variety of other influences are involved, including the ways that electronic grading systems are programmed, ancient administrative policies, accidental errors, and teachers' and administrators' idiosyncratic judgments. If a school system aspires to implement a grading system that is fair, accurate, specific, and timely, then it must create grading mechanisms that focus more on students' performance and less on subjective factors unrelated to student achievement.

Let us begin with the premise that people want to be successful. Students want to learn, teachers want their students to excel, and education leaders and policymakers make their decisions in pursuit of students' best interests. Teachers also want their students to arrive in class ready to learn, finish their assigned work, respect teacher feedback, and leave at the end of the year ready to enter the next level of learning with confidence and success. When we assume goodwill by students, teachers, and leaders, we influence even the most difficult discussions in a positive way. Rather than presume that we must convert bad teachers into barely acceptable ones, let's instead focus on how to help excellent teachers, administrators, board members, students, and parents make better decisions about one of the most important and emotional subjects in education—how to grade to promote improved student performance.

Of course, grading is only one form of feedback, but it is the form that gets the most attention. Guskey and Bailey (2001) argue that feedback other than grading is actually more influential on student learning. This contention makes sense. Consider, for example, how effective feedback from coaches and music teachers results in encouragement, corrections, and immediate improvement. If a school has an excellent system of feedback but ineffective grading practices, that school undermines many of its own efforts. However, if a school is able to implement effective grading practices, it reinforces all of its other educational endeavors.

Reconciling Experience and Evidence

We are all victims of experience and context, often believing that personal experience is superior to evidence. While students have learned to scoff at medieval superstitions and to value the testing of hypotheses, prevailing discussions in education often remain stubbornly focused on experience rather than evidence.

Casual assertions have a way of becoming accepted with insufficient challenge. Some readers might recall futurists of the 1980s predicting that by the year 2000 schools would be paperless and student writing would give way to dictation into voice-recognition systems. As we know, neither prediction is close to reality. Educators still endure similar assertions about their profession and about grading policies. Rhetorical certitude, however, is not a substitute for evidence. When considering how to improve grading policies, one of the most important agreements that teachers, parents, students, and school leaders must reach is that evidence should guide their conclusions.

Try an experiment with your colleagues by asking them the following questions.

- What enduring principles have you learned in your career? What, in brief, do you know for sure about teaching, learning, and student achievement?

- What beliefs did you have ten years ago that you now know are no longer true?

Compare the quantity of responses to the first question to the quantity of responses to the second question. I rarely have difficulty eliciting a conclusion to the first question: "The primary causes of student achievement are . . ." or "The most important components of good teaching are . . ." However, the responses to the second question require some effort. Admitting that what we knew a decade ago in education was imprecise, uncertain, or downright wrong appears to require a rare degree of candor.

Now, pose the same questions to an ophthalmologist, climatologist, marine biologist, cardiologist, orthopedic surgeon, or international aid worker. These professionals have little difficulty acknowledging that what they know today surpasses what they knew in previous decades. They accept the fact that today's evidence trumps yesterday's experience. For example, a cardiac surgeon knows that twelve years spent in a surgical residency taught her very little about the powerful effects of behavioral modification on heart patients today. That doesn't undermine the value of her surgical training but rather amplifies the value. Each time we know—as parents, professionals, craftsmen, musicians, or students—a little bit more about how our work improves and the results we expect, the better our results will be.

Thankfully, the use of evidence in medicine and many other fields has led to meaningful and life-saving reforms (McAfee, 2009). The elevation of personal preference over evidence is not unique to education but appears to be part of human nature. It seems people prefer the comfort of the familiar over the discomfort of the new, even if evidence supports the latter. That is why the most rational and reasonable people can do irrational and unreasonable things in resisting change (Deutschman, 2007). However clear the evidence, personal experience remains triumphant in too many discussions of education policy.

Education in particular—a profession that prides itself on progress—is rooted deeply in past convictions. We lay claim to 21st century learning by placing an electronic board at the front of the class, but we lecture as if electricity has not yet been invented. We praise collaboration yet often assess our students in a manner that punishes and berates peer assistance.

How can we distinguish experience from evidence? The most effective way I know is to use the following six levels of evidence.

1. **Opinion:** "This is what I believe, and I believe it sincerely."

2. **Experience:** "This is what I have learned based on my personal observation."

3. **Local evidence:** "This is what I have learned based on the evidence, which not only includes my own experience but also my friends' and colleagues' experiences."

4. **Systematic observation:** "I have compared twelve schools that fully implemented my proposed intervention with twelve schools that did not implement it. Here are the results that show the difference between these twenty-four schools . . ."

5. **Preponderance of evidence:** "This is what we know as a profession based on many of our colleagues' systematic observations in many different circumstances in varied locations and at many different times."

6. **Mathematical certainty:** "Two plus two equals four, and we really don't need to take a vote on whether that statement is agreeable to everyone."

In a world subject to relativism in every sense—political, moral, and even scientific and mathematical—certainty seems elusive, particularly in regard to controversial topics like education practices. Nevertheless, there is an appropriate place for the definitive language of mathematics in our approach to grading. For example, when teachers use the mean, or average, to calculate a student's grade, they reach a different mathematical result than when they focus on the student's final scores. When teachers use a 0 on a one hundred–point scale, they reach a different mathematical result than when they use a 0 on a four-point scale. These are not matters of conjecture but simple calculation.

The first step toward reconciling debate in education, or any other matter of public policy, is for the rhetorical combatants to be intellectually honest about their claims and capable of distinguishing among what they believe, what they see, what they hear from colleagues, and what they have learned from the evidence.

Conversations About Change

There are two ways to begin a conversation with classroom teachers and building administrators about changing practices. The first is characterized by one-sided enthusiasm. Zealous advocates who adopt this method typically have goodwill, good research, and good intentions, but their audiences soon move from boredom to frustration to active opposition. What began as a collegial conversation focused on questions of practical application ultimately becomes entrenched opposition. Yesterday's reasonable challenge becomes tomorrow's grievances. Thoughtful dialogue and professional conversation are transformed into rancor. Colleagues become opponents, with each side wondering, "Haven't we been down this road before?"

The second way to begin the conversation is with a question, not a statement. Rather than telling teachers and administrators what they need to do, we can ask, "What prevents you from being the very best teacher and administrator you can be?" The following are common responses to that question.

- "The kids don't care."
- "The parents don't care."
- "Many of the students don't come to school."
- "Students who do come to school are disengaged, inattentive, preoccupied, and angry."
- "Administrators don't support teachers who demand quality student work."
- "Leaders at the system level tolerate poor teachers and administrators."
- "Colleagues won't cooperate and collaborate."

The list could go on and on. Nevertheless, it is definitely a question worth asking.

This book is not a prescription. Rather, it poses a number of important questions and suggests the creation of boundaries. For example, in athletics, each contest has boundaries. No strategy, no matter how creative, is acceptable if it takes place outside of those boundaries. Officials, coaches, and athletes know the boundaries of their sport well. Within them are the thrill of victory and the agony of defeat. Outside of them is the zone of irrelevance. The elements of this book act as four essential boundaries for grading—remember the useful acronym *FAST*.

1. **Grades must be fair.** Gender, ethnicity, socioeconomic status, political attitudes, or other factors unrelated to academic performance must not influence grades.

2. **Grades must be accurate.** Grades must reflect the student's performance.

3. **Grades must be specific.** Grades not only are an evaluation but also feedback. Students, parents, and teachers must understand the grade and also have sufficiently specific information so they can use the teacher's feedback to improve student performance.

4. **Grades must be timely.** While there is, inevitably, a final grade that appears on an official transcript, particularly in secondary school, that is but a postscript to a very long story. Much earlier than the final grade, students should receive a steady stream of feedback, similar to what athletes receive from coaches, designed not merely to evaluate their performance but to improve it.

Fairness, accuracy, specificity, and timeliness—these elements are the criteria for building effective grading polices, and these are the topics explored in the pages of this book.

What's New in the Second Edition

Since the first edition of *Elements of Grading*, the controversies surrounding grading practices have not been resolved but rather have escalated. The development of Twitter and the active international participation in #SBLChat (for standards-based learning) has highlighted the difficulty in establishing systemwide reform. The common themes in these discussions are that teachers who are committed to standards-based grading are largely working in isolation in an environment actively hostile to grading reform. Therefore, in the second edition, I have not only added more about the grading debate but also who should be engaged in that debate. This not only includes teachers and administrators but also parents, skeptics, and the general public.

Moreover, we must be aware of grading reform ideas that have failed—the "minimum 50" is a good example of this. In an attempt to save students from the impact of a 0 on a one hundred–point scale, some schools have tried to implement a minimum grade of 50. However, this policy runs into almost universal opposition because, critics reason, "Why should a student earn fifty points for doing nothing? If I came to work half the time, I wouldn't get half the pay!" The second edition provides more simple and palatable reforms that answer the most basic challenges of critics: students can continue to receive letter grades; they still have a transcript for admission to college; parents have clear and accurate information about the academic progress of their children; and teachers have the professional discretion to award grades based on student proficiency rather than a computerized conclusion that may be far from the teacher's judgment.

The second edition also includes sections on the impact of technology on grading practices, grading in the context of the Common Core State Standards, student engagement, and grading for students with special needs. Finally, this edition offers an international perspective, as public and private educational systems around the globe are dealing with the issue of improving grading policies. I hope that this book provides a source of study and guidance for faculties and administrators as they seek the best grading solutions for their schools and education systems.

Chapter 1

EFFECTIVE GRADING IN A STANDARDS-BASED WORLD

This is the paradox of standards-based education: education systems around the world widely accept standards in theory. The official embrace of standards-based education has grown dramatically, from only a dozen states adopting standards to all fifty states, along with many education systems around the world, including Norway, Malaysia, Japan, Australia, the Philippines, Turkey, the United Arab Emirates, Mexico, Chile, and Canada, to name a few (International Society for Technology in Education, 2015). While the standards certainly vary, including academic, technology, and teacher qualification standards, the principle of standards-based reform is global in scope.

There are surely differences regarding which standards to adopt, with much contention about the use of Common Core State Standards. Nevertheless, the central controversy involves which standards to adopt, not whether or not standards should be adopted. Despite the illusion of consensus about the value of academic standards, the reality is that standards in practice—particularly in the ways that teachers evaluate students—have been stubbornly indifferent to change. Education systems embracing 21st century standards with breathless enthusiasm continue to implement grading practices firmly rooted in the 19th century.

This chapter explores what standards mean for grading practices and policies, considers the advantages and criticisms of standards, and offers some practical advice about using standards to influence improved grading practices.

What Standards-Based Education Really Means

There are two common ways to evaluate students. We can compare their performance to other students, or we can compare their performance to an objective standard. The first method, comparing students to one another, makes sense when one must allocate a scarce resource, such as admission to highly selective colleges. However, this method makes no sense when the stakes are really high, such as landing an airliner or performing brain surgery. In these examples, it is not enough to merely be better than one's peers. Rather, it is essential that the pilot and the surgeon meet a standard—our second way to evaluate students. The claim that an airline doesn't crash as frequently as other airlines or that a hospital has fewer deaths than the hospital across town provides scant reassurance to passengers and patients. What the public cares about is not who beat whom but rather the degree of proficiency pilots and surgeons possess.

The essentials of standards are the same for students as for pilots and surgeons. When we compare students to one another, we have the worst of all possible worlds. This system regards students who have mastered standards as inadequate if it has assessed another student in the class as better. Worse yet, it labels students who have failed to master a standard as excellent, as long as they are superior to their peers.

Is the comparison of student performance to pilots and surgeons overwrought? Not if you consider the impact of student failure on health and social well-being. As Alliance for Excellent Education (2010) research indicates, students who fail in school have dramatically higher medical care costs, lower incomes, and disproportionate use of the criminal justice system. Failures in the cockpit and surgical suite not only affect the people directly involved but all of society. Similarly, failures in the classroom affect all of us.

Standards are a delusion if students are not evaluated on their proficiency. Despite the public embrace of standards since the 1990s, standards-based student evaluation has been slow to develop. While researching this book, I interviewed some of the most prominent international leaders in education reform. Most claim that although there are occasional exceptions, very few examples exist in classrooms or schools in which an entire education system backs up its rhetoric of standards with the reality of standards-based student evaluation.

What Makes Standards-Based Grading Different

Imagine that you are teaching your teenage son to drive. You have selected a deserted parking lot on a Sunday morning where very little could go wrong. You relinquish the driver's seat and make sure that your seat belts are so tight that they almost constrict your breathing. As your teen driver lurches forward, you notice that most of the parking lot lampposts bear the scars of car paint. It appears that you are not the first person who thought that the parking lot would be a good training ground for new drivers.

There are two possible questions that you can consider. The first is, "Will my kid make fewer dents in the lampposts (and the family car) than the last dozen teenage drivers who were here?" That sort of thinking sets the bar dangerously low. The second question is, "What does my teenager need to do in order to become a safe and proficient driver?" This is what Jay McTighe and Grant Wiggins (2013) might call an essential question. Essential questions are those that not only require merely a binary response but also a deep inquiry into the thought processes behind the question.

What do teenage drivers and academic standards have in common? Consider the case of Princeton University. This is home to a lot of very smart people, including Nobel Prize–winning faculty members and a student body that includes some of the most talented and intelligent young people the world has to offer. These students already know how to earn great marks in school. The reason they came to Princeton was not to accumulate more As on their transcripts but to engage in life-changing intellectual challenges. But even very smart people can make critical mistakes. Persuaded that Princetonians were getting by too easily, the university decided to limit the number of A grades to 35 percent of a class (Ad Hoc Committee to Review Policies Regarding Assessment and Grading, 2014). The idea that 65 percent of Princeton students were incapable of earning an A is mind-boggling. Nevertheless, this example is at the heart of what makes standards-based grading different. Grading based on the bell curve assumes that some people meet standards, very few people exceed the standards, and half of people fail to meet the standards. Standards-based grading, by contrast, allows any student—indeed, the vast majority of students—to meet academic standards as long they demonstrate proficiency in those standards.

The mirror image of the Princeton example is the case of students who receive honor roll grades but are unable to meet basic literacy requirements (Reeves, 2006a). These students are quiet and never speak out of turn or challenge a teacher and receive good grades as a reward, while teachers punish their more boisterous peers for challenging and engaging behaviors.

The fundamental characteristic of standards-based grading is that students are evaluated based on an objective measure of performance—don't hit the lamppost; don't plagiarize your senior thesis; and provide work that is, after much trial and error, a significant intellectual achievement when compared to objective criteria. The alternative is a stark contrast—it's OK to hit the lamppost, but don't hit it as frequently as the last student driving in this parking lot. It's OK to plagiarize, as long as you don't do it as much as the last student who got caught. Finally, your intellectual contributions don't need to be thoughtful and creative, as long as they are not as thickheaded as the last thousand papers the professor has endured. While critics of standards-based grading complain that it sets the bar too low because too many students can succeed, precisely the opposite is true. It is comparative grading, typically based on the normal distribution, or bell curve.

Finally, to be fair to Princeton, it is noteworthy that the document cited previously explains that the university changed its grading policy back to allowing faculty determination of proficiency, not the bell curve, to determine student grades.

What the Critics Say

Standards, along with standards-based grading, are not without their critics. There are critics from both ends of the political spectrum who, while disagreeing on nearly every other element of education policy, are united in their condemnation of standards and standards-based grading. Two of the leading critics of standards are Diane Ravitch of New York University (http://dianeravitch.com) and Yong Zhao of the University of Oregon (http://zhaolearning.com).

Professor Ravitch is particularly critical of the relationship between standards and the misuse of standardized testing—the connection between corporate test vendors and standards-based accountability. She rightly contends that school reform has never been achieved through threats and intimidation and has offered devastating critiques of those who magnify the deficiencies of schools. But it is important to separate the argument from the implications. There is broad agreement among researchers that standardized testing—particularly when used in a high-stakes environment to threaten students and teachers—has been a grossly ineffective and an unreliable tool. In fact, it is counterproductive (Guskey, 2015).

When teachers are threatened with termination on the basis of standardized test results, the result is not necessarily an improvement in teaching and learning but a migration of teachers from low-performing systems to high-performing systems. This phenomenon leaves low-performing schools with a dearth of the best teachers and provides students who most need excellent instruction with an annual merry-go-round of new and inexperienced teachers, along with veterans who were unable to get a job elsewhere.

This does not deny the fact that there are excellent and dedicated teachers laboring in low-performing schools, but the overwhelming evidence is that these are the exceptions (Haycock & Crawford, 2008). The faculties and administrations of low-performing schools are largely populated by a revolving door of professionals who, no matter how dedicated, know that the performance of their school could doom their careers, and they seek to leave as soon as possible.

In essence, Ravitch's criticisms of standards are not so much an objection to the establishment of academic standards but rather their ill-advised use for standardized testing and the resulting enrichment of test vendors.

A different criticism of standards comes from Zhao (2014), who contends that all standards represent a totalitarian influence on education. He not only objects to the Common Core and other versions of academic standards but to all standards. The elevation of literacy, for example, denies students the opportunity to pursue their interest in physical education or creative arts. Susan Ohanian (1999) joins Zhao in this general opposition.

Standards critics also include political groups who oppose any set of external standards as an imposition on local control, a term that varies widely in its implication. For some critics, a careful reading of the Tenth Amendment requires that powers not enumerated in the Constitution be reserved to the states (National Constitution Center, 2015). For others, local control means that all education requirements are the exclusive province of the local school board. For others, the same term implies that teachers rule the classroom domain and that they are best equipped to determine the curriculum, assessment, academic standards, and grading policies and practices for their classrooms.

Critics make strange bedfellows. It would be foolhardy to ignore these critics, however disparate their reasoning might be. Too often, discourse, especially political discourse, is conducted in an echo chamber in which we only consider the views of those with whom we agree, while ignoring differing opinions. The successful implementation of effective grading policies requires thoughtful and respectful engagement with critics, including all ends of the political spectrum, teachers, parents, and policymakers.

How to Separate Policy From Politics

How can we bridge the gap between the advocates and critics of standards? The first and most important consideration is to find common ground. In every education debate, it might be a good start to stipulate that those who disagree with us are neither evil nor indifferent to student needs. We can respect people of sincere goodwill who favor government intervention to support educational opportunities for all students as well as those who favor limited government and oppose any federal or state intrusion into school matters, no matter how well intentioned.

In such a politically charged environment, where is the common ground? You might find it on a Friday night at your local high school football, basketball, or volleyball game. Parents, teachers, administrators, and board members of wildly different political persuasions can agree on a few things, aside from the fact that their team is the best on the field. Where do we find common ground in athletics (or interscholastic competitions in science, music, art, debate, poetry, and many other fields)? Can we compare the judgments in athletics to those in standards-based grading? How do they compare? Again, the judgments must be FAST.

First, we agree that judgments must be fair. By fair, we mean that the same behavior merits the same reward or penalty. For example, when one team engages in flagrant rule violations, whether it is unnecessary roughness on the football field or going overtime in a speech competition, fair judgment requires that all competitors who engage in the same violation receive the same penalty. The histrionics of World Cup players notwithstanding, it is not the pleading of the players that determines the officials' judgment but rather an objective view of the players' conduct. The research in this book demonstrates that effective grading practices, particularly those based on standards, are more likely to be fair. Even the fiercest critics of standards might agree that fairness is a noble objective, even if it comes from different political perspectives.

Second, we agree the judgments must be accurate. By accurate we mean that assessments of student performance are based solely on the performance itself and not the heredity, wealth, or status of the student. In this book, I argue that standards-based grading is much more likely to be accurate than comparative grading. But even for people who disagree with that proposition, I hope that we can all agree that accuracy is a good thing.

Third, we agree that judgments must be specific. Under the bright lights of a Friday night game, the officials do not announce "Bad play!" or "Rule violation!" Rather, they state with specificity what the infraction was, such as "Offsides!" or "Illegal formation!" The specific imperative is hardly limited to athletic competitions. In fields as diverse as science and the creative arts, specificity is at the heart of encouraging improved performance.

Fourth, and lastly, we can agree that judgments must be timely. The requirement for timely judgments is inextricably linked to the requirement for specificity. With ambiguous rules, judgments would take the entire weekend. With specific rules, however, we must make judgments so the game ends before midnight. The fundamental reason for timely judgments is not the convenience of the observers or participants but rather the educational imperative that students use feedback to improve performance. If I know that I was offsides on the last play, I am less likely to make the same mistake on the next play.

These attempts to find common ground are not naïve. In the landmark study of negotiation, *Getting to Yes* (Fisher & Ury, 2011), even the most disputatious opponents can begin the process of negotiating an end to their quarrels when they first find common ground. It is true that the most hard-core opponents of civil conversation will not agree on these four principles. "What is fairness?" they might inquire. "It's all in the eye of the beholder!" The possibility that some people will not engage in civil conversation does not absolve the rest of us from attempting rational engagement. The alternative, as grading controversies since well before the 21st century have shown, is gridlock. The adults involved in fierce advocacy never win, but students certainly lose.

How Standards Impact Grading

It doesn't matter whether you are participating in the Common Core State Standards; state, provincial, or national standards; or standards established by your own school or local education system. The central issue in transforming policy into practice is not the standards' authorship or source but rather their application to student performance as the basis for evaluation.

The impact of standards on grading practices includes the following three hallmarks.

1. **Student performance is compared to objective standards:** It is possible for every student in the class to earn a top mark and similarly possible for no students to achieve top marks. There is no requirement for a certain number of As, and there is no requirement for a certain number of students to perform below that level. The only criterion that matters is performance. For example, officers administering student driving tests are not required to issue passing or failing marks to a certain percentage of students every day. Instead, they compare the performance of their student drivers to objective standards.

2. **The rationale behind student evaluations is clear:** The essential question is not "What grade did I get?" but rather "How do I get to the next level of performance?" For example, I overheard two fifth-grade students who, in only their second week of school, were talking about their forthcoming report cards—two months away. The school uses a four-point scale to describe performance.

    One student commented, "I'm OK with getting a 3, but I wish that they would tell me what I need to do to move to a 4." It's a fair challenge. In a standards-based grading system, the answer is crystal clear. In writing, for example, a student might say, "I earned a 3 because I wrote really good paragraphs that have clear topic sentences and supporting details. But if I want to earn a 4, I need to use more powerful vocabulary and have a stronger closing paragraph." In mathematics, the student might say, "I earned a 2 because I got most of the answers right, but I really didn't explain how I got them. I need to ask for help to get to the next level. Even though I think I know some of the answers, I'm not sure why they are right. I need to practice explaining my work." In brief, whatever the level of the student, the key to effective standards-based grading, in practice, is that students can articulate their present level of learning and explain in their own words what they need to do in order to advance to the next level.

3. **School- and district-level administrators model clear expectations for teachers, and teachers model clear expectations for students:** For example, if they expect teachers to provide specific and timely feedback to students, then administrators must do the same after every formal and informal classroom observation. There must be no mystery about what a walkthrough or other observation means. Administrators must be clear about their criteria, for example, "This week, I'm going to be observing classrooms with a focus on feedback. In particular, I'm going to focus on the number of students who receive feedback from the teacher and, most importantly, the number of students who use that feedback to make immediate improvements in their performance."

We do not have to agree on standards in order to embrace effective grading practices. The key to applying effective grading practices is not which standards you use but how you apply the standards that you choose to give fair, accurate, specific, and timely feedback to students.

The next chapter explores what the CCSS mean for grading.

Chapter 2

WHAT THE COMMON CORE MEANS FOR GRADING

For the most part, states have become ambivalent about the Common Core, although initially almost every state embraced this effort, which the National Governors Association Center for Best Practices (NGA) and the Council of Chief State School Officers (CCSSO) support. At the writing of this book, however, the support has dwindled to about two-thirds of the states, and many state legislative chambers are clamoring for disengagement from the Common Core and the tests associated with it (Bidwell, 2014).

If you are reading this book in a state where the Common Core is not embraced or supported, you can certainly skip this chapter. But I'd like to suggest that these few pages might be worthwhile reading for any educator, administrator, or policymaker. The reason is that every set of standards—from the fifty separate state standards at the onset of the 21st century to the provincial curricula in Canada to the International Baccalaureate (IB) curricula and virtually any other state of academic expectations—has some elements in common with regard to teaching, learning, and assessing. Most importantly, an effective grading system supports many of these alternative curriculum frameworks. An ineffective grading system, however, undermines even the best academic expectations. Therefore, whether your school is committed to the Common Core State Standards, drifting away from them, or virulently opposed to them, there remains something to learn about the relationship between effective grading practices and the Common Core.

What the Common Core Says—and Doesn't Say

The Common Core says what to teach, not how to teach it. In fact, it really doesn't even do a complete job of saying what to teach because the Common Core is not a curriculum. The learning expectations are clear, and although there are many suggested ideas for classroom teachers, there is no national reading list, no list of writing prompts that every teacher must use, no curriculum that is standardized in every classroom, and certainly no list of effective teaching practices (NGA & CCSSO, 2010a, 2010b). The decisions about how to test, how frequently to test, and which tests to use firmly remain each state's prerogative. Although many states have made commitments, through the receipt of federal Race to the Top grants, a growing number of states have defied the federal government as it attempts to enforce commitments made when those grants were being pursued.

How the Common Core Influences Teaching

Although the Common Core does not specify how to teach, the academic expectations within the Common Core certainly should influence many classroom practices. Foremost among these influences is the significant increase in the quantity and quality of classroom writing. In particular, the Common Core shifts the focus of classroom writing from personal narrative and creative writing to descriptive, analytical, and argumentative writing. Certainly there remains space for poetry, creative essays, and personal narratives in the curriculum. But in order to meet the writing requirements of the Common Core, almost every teacher in every discipline needs to make student writing a much greater part of the curriculum.

Another important influence of the Common Core on teaching practices is the increase in the use of scoring guides, or rubrics, to assess student performance. The documents supporting the Common Core provide many examples of scoring guides (NGA & CSSD, n.d.). Of particular help are student work examples featured on the Common Core website, which correspond to each level of performance. This encourages, but does not require, teachers to incorporate the explicit feedback of scoring guides into their daily practice.

By using these guides, teachers tend to be more explicit and consistent in their expectations, and students know what they must do in order to improve their performance. Most importantly, teachers' expectations regarding student performance are linked explicitly to a set of standards and not to individual teachers' idiosyncratic expectations. This is a good idea for any set of academic expectations, whether they are the Common Core State Standards or an alternative.

How the Common Core Influences Assessment

The Common Core, like any set of standards, focuses student learning on proficiency as measured against an objective standard. When all students are proficient, then it is possible that all students pass an assessment. When no students are proficient, then it is possible that no students pass an assessment. If the assessment accurately reflects the standards, then the response to low student performance is not to change the test or criticize the standards but simply to get feedback on how each student performed and how he or she can work harder and retake the assessment.

Schools know how to do this. They don't widen the goal posts in soccer when too few goals are scored, and they don't lower the height of the basket when basketball scores are low. Schools know how to get feedback, use it, work hard, and improve performance. The great question as the Common Core proceeds and, understandably, student results are lower than expected (this typically happens when more rigorous standards are implemented and less familiar test items are used), is what the reactions will be from educators, school leaders, policymakers, and parents (Linn, 1998). They might say, "It's obvious that the assessment is flawed. Our kids can't be that bad!" Or, they might say, "Since we have agreed to a path of more rigorous standards, it looks as if we have some work to do in order to move student performance to a higher level." Watch the political rhetoric in the years ahead to see which path your jurisdiction takes.

How the Common Core Influences Grading

Although the Common Core State Standards do not contain a syllable about grading, the influence of these standards on grading is unmistakable if they are implemented faithfully. It is illogical, for example, to apply the standards and conclude that a student is proficient and then give that student failing marks for reasons not related to the academic standards. The Common Core doesn't say a word about homework, extra credit, or attendance, all common elements of grading practices that have a major impact on evaluating the success and failure of students. All of these criteria and more remain the exclusive purview of teachers, schools, and systems.

Although the Common Core influences many matters related to what students should know and be able to do, it is completely silent on one of the greatest influences on student success—feedback and grading. Therefore, whatever standards your school chooses to use, your choice of grading practices remains one of the most important decisions you can make when it comes to improving student achievement.

Whatever the future of the Common Core, enduring influences on student achievement can be immune from the vagaries of political winds. These include feedback, an exceptionally strong influence on student achievement. The next chapter explores feedback and grading, which are inextricably linked. Parents and students do not ask about the details of standards but rather, "What's the grade?" If we want a meaningful answer to that question, then we must provide effective feedback throughout the school year.

Chapter 3

THE IMPACT OF FEEDBACK ON ACHIEVEMENT

Although grading policies can be the subject of deeply held opinions, debates about grading are more constructive if we first agree on two important premises. First, we should be willing to agree that grading is a form of feedback. Second, we should be willing to agree that feedback is a very powerful instructional technique—some would say the most powerful—when it comes to influencing student achievement.

Evaluating the Evidence

Let's look at the evidence. John Hattie's (2009) synthesis of more than eight hundred meta-analyses evaluates the relative impact of many factors, including family structure, curriculum, teaching practices, and feedback on student achievement. The measurement that Hattie uses is effect size, or, simply put, the effectiveness of particular interventions. The impact of an effect size of 0.4 is, according to Hattie, about one year of learning. Therefore, any instructional or leadership initiative must at least pass this threshold. Many factors are statistically significant, as the following list will show. But statistical significance and practical significance are two different elements. Because of the overwhelming burdens on the time and resources of every school (Reeves, 2011a), it makes little sense to invest in initiatives that fail to cross the 0.4 level in effect size. An effect size of 1.0, Hattie suggests, would be blatantly obvious, such as the difference between two people who are 5 feet 3 inches (160 cm) and 6 feet (183 cm) in height—a difference clearly observable.

Even small effect sizes can be meaningful, particularly if they are devoted to initiatives that save lives. For example, Robert Rosenthal and M. Robin DiMatteo (2001) demonstrate that the effect size of taking a low dose of aspirin in preventing a heart attack is 0.07—a small fraction of a standard deviation—yet this translates into the result that thirty-four out of every one thousand people would be saved from a heart attack by using a low dose of aspirin on a regular basis.

The use of the common statistic for effect size helps busy teachers and school administrators evaluate alternative strategies and their impact on achievement compared to variables outside teachers' and students' control. For example, some of Hattie's findings include the influence of the following on student achievement (Hattie, 2009).

- Preterm birth weight (0.54)
- Illness (0.23)
- Diet (0.12)
- Drug use (0.33)
- Exercise (0.28)
- Socioeconomic status (0.57)
- Family structure (0.17)
- Home environment (0.57)
- Parental involvement (0.51)

Most teachers would view these factors as outside of their control, although some would certainly argue that schools can do a better job of influencing diet, drug use, exercise, and parental involvement. During the eighteen hours every day that students are not in school, students and families make many decisions that influence learning in significant ways. But how important are these decisions compared to the variables that teachers and school administrators can control?

The Importance of Feedback

The effectiveness of any recommendation regarding teaching and education leadership depends on the extent to which the professional practices of educators and school leaders have a greater impact on students than factors that are beyond their control. The essential question is, Will this idea have a sufficient impact in helping students overcome any negative influences they face outside of school?

Fortunately, Hattie (2009) answers that question with a resounding affirmative response. He finds a number of teaching and leadership practices that, measured in the synthesis of meta-analyses, are more powerful than personality, home, and demographic factors when considering their impact on student achievement. Examples include teacher-student relationships (0.72), professional development (0.62), teacher clarity (0.75), vocabulary programs (0.67), creativity programs (0.65), and feedback (0.73).

Certainly, Hattie is not the first scholar to recognize the importance of feedback on student achievement. His findings are completely consistent with Robert Marzano's (2007, 2010) conclusions that accurate, specific, and timely feedback is linked to student learning. Thanks to Hattie's research, however, we can now be more precise than ever about how important it is. We can say that, based on the preponderance of evidence from multiple studies in many cultural settings, feedback is not only more important than most other instructional interventions but is also more important than socioeconomic status, drug use, nutrition, exercise, anxiety, family structure, and a host of other factors that many people claim are overwhelming. Indeed, when it comes to evaluating the relative impact of what teachers and education leaders do, the combined use of formative evaluation and feedback is the most powerful combination that we have. If we understand that a grade is not just an evaluation process but also one of the most important forms of feedback that students can receive, Hattie's conclusion should elevate the improvement of grading policies to a top priority in every school.

Hattie (2009) also encourages a broadly based view of feedback, including feedback not only from teachers to students but also from teachers to their colleagues. We should recall that, as a fundamental ethical principle, no student in a school should be more accountable than the adults, and thus our feedback systems must be as appropriate for teachers and leaders as they are for students. Similarly, our standards for administrators, board members, and policymakers must be at least as rigorous as those we create for fourth graders. If that statement seems astonishing, then I invite you to obtain a copy of the fourth-grade academic standards for your area and lay beside them the standards that are officially endorsed for policymakers, such as legislators, members of parliament, members of Congress, or other educational authorities. You can then decide which standards are more demanding.

The Evidence–Decision Gap

It is therefore mystifying that a strategy with so great an impact on student achievement as feedback remains so controversial and inconsistent. It is as if there was evidence that a common consumer practice created an environmental disaster, but people ignored it and persisted in the destructive practice. Of course, that is hardly a hypothetical example, as our national habits—such as persistent use of bottled water, dependence on gas-guzzling cars, and appetite for junk food—illustrate. Rather than embrace the evidence and use filtered tap water, take public transportation, and eat fresh vegetables, we often choose the convenient alternatives that are less healthy for our families and the planet.

In sum, our greatest challenge is how to transform what we know into action. Indifference to research, though also present in medicine, business, and many other fields (Pfeffer & Sutton, 2006a), is particularly striking in education. An alarming example is the persistent use of retention and corporal punishment. In both cases, decades of evidence suggest that these "treatments" are inversely related to student learning. Retention does not encourage work ethic and student responsibility but only creates older, frustrated, and less successful students (Hattie, 2009). Corporal punishment does not improve behavior but legitimizes violence and increases bullying and student misbehavior (Committee on School Health, 2000). Nevertheless, politicians from all parties have excoriated social promotion and urged retention in a display of belligerent indifference to the evidence. More disturbingly, nineteen states and many other nations continue to permit corporal punishment decades after the evidence concluded it was counterproductive (Strauss, 2014).

Equipped with rich literature on the theory and practice of change, educators and school leaders should be fully capable of acknowledging error, evaluating alternatives, testing alternative hypotheses, and drawing conclusions that lead to better results. Instead, personal convictions that are not only antiquated but maybe even dangerous guide decision-making processes. We can be indignant about the physicians of the 19th century who were unwilling to wash their hands, but when the subject turns to education policies, we sometimes elevate prejudice over evidence.

Before we consider what quality feedback is, let us be clear about what feedback is not. Feedback is not testing.

Distinguishing Feedback From Testing

Consider two classrooms, both burdened by large class sizes and students with a wide range of background knowledge and skill levels. The role of the teacher in the first class is to deliver what, as a matter of school-system policy, has been described as a "guaranteed curriculum." Administrators know that the curriculum is delivered because teachers list the instructional objectives on the board and post the details of the lesson plan supporting those objectives next to the door, where visiting leaders can easily inspect them. In this class, the most important feedback that students and teachers receive is on the annual test administered every spring. This feedback is very detailed, as it determines the success and failure of not only individual students but also the entire school, perhaps the entire school system. Moreover, external companies have established elaborate statistical formulas that give feedback to individual teachers, measuring the degree to which each teacher is adding value to each student.

When comparing students over three years, these analyses conclude that teachers whose students show gains in test scores have added value to their students, whereas teachers whose students do not make such gains have failed to add value. So ingrained is this sort of analysis that in the United States, one of the conditions states must meet in order to be competitive for federal funds is the commitment to link teacher evaluation to annual measures in student performance.

There is no question that annual tests are important, if by important we mean that decisions involving the lives of students, teachers, and school administrators, along with billions of taxpayer dollars, are influenced by those tests. Ask the teacher and students in the first class how they know when they are succeeding, and the answer is, almost uniformly, "We'll know when we get our state test results back." However, the question at hand is whether these test results really provide feedback.

The second class is no less rigorous than the first. Indeed, it can be argued that this class is more rigorous. The teacher provides informal feedback to students every day, and each week students update their learning logs to identify where they are with respect to their learning targets and next steps for moving forward. Students, along with the teacher, are continuously assessing their learning but not with a single standardized test. Moreover, the teacher in the second class assesses skills that are never tested by the state, including collaboration, critical thinking, creativity, and communication. This teacher is not assessing less but assessing more to prepare students not only for the state test but also for the broader requirements students will encounter in the years ahead.

Reconsidering Feedback

In her landmark work comparing high- and low-performing nations and high- and low-performing state education systems, Linda Darling-Hammond (2010) comes to an astonishing and counterintuitive conclusion. Since the 1980s, the three exemplars she considers—Singapore, South Korea, and Finland—made significant progress according to international education comparisons over the next three decades. More than 90 percent of the students in these countries graduate from high school, and large majorities go to college—"far more than in the much wealthier United States" (p. 192), Darling-Hammond concludes. Detailed field observations reveal the rich, nuanced feedback that students and teachers receive daily and can apply immediately.

"Wait," you may say. "Don't Asian countries like South Korea and Singapore also have a test-focused environment? Aren't those the examples that we tried to emulate to improve our academic performance in mathematics and science?" In fact, this does not comport with Darling-Hammond's (2010) evidence. These successful nations:

> *eliminated examination systems* that had previously tracked students for middle schools and restricted access to high school. Finland and Korea now have no external examinations before the voluntary matriculation exams for college. In addition to the "O" level matriculation examinations, students in Singapore take examinations at the end of primary school (grade 6), which are used to calculate value-added contributions to their learning that are part of the information system about secondary schools. These examinations require extensive written responses and problem solving, and include curriculum-embedded projects and papers that are graded by teachers. (p. 192, emphasis in original)

Effective education systems certainly use some system-level examinations, but notice the important distinctions. In these examples, even national examinations include deep teacher involvement and, therefore, offer the opportunity for feedback that is far more nuanced than a simple score. Most importantly, the vast majority of feedback is in the daily interactions between students and teachers, not from test scores administered at multiyear intervals. Perhaps the most important consideration is how teachers and students evaluate their own success. While annual high-stakes testing leaves students and teachers wondering about their success ("We'll know how we're doing when we see the scores at the end of the year"), a system characterized by effective feedback offers a dramatically different view.

Darling-Hammond (2010) observes the dramatic difference between the feedback as testing model and the feedback as breathing model, with the latter characterized by feedback integral to the minute-to-minute reality of the classroom. The following words are not from a veteran teacher, nor are they from the graduate of a top-tier teacher-preparation program with several years of intensive mentoring. They are the words of a prospective teacher who was fortunate enough to see Darling-Hammond's (2010) fieldwork but had not yet spent a day in the classroom. This teacher says:

> For me the most valuable thing was the sequencing of the lessons, teaching the lesson, and evaluating what the kids were getting, what the kids weren't getting, and having that be reflected in my next lesson . . . the "teach-assess-teach-assess-teach-assess" process. (as cited in Darling-Hammond, 2010, p. 223)

Bridget Hamre of the University of Virginia Curry School of Education notes that "high-quality feedback is where there is a back-and-forth exchange to get a deeper understanding" (as cited in Gladwell, 2009, p. 326). Bob Pianta, dean of the Curry School, reports on what a team he led observed in a class with high levels of interactive feedback:

> "So let's see," [the teacher] began, standing up at the blackboard. "Special right triangles. We're going to do practice with this, just throwing out ideas." He drew two triangles. "Label the length of the side, if you can. If you can't, we'll all do it." He was talking and moving quickly, which Pianta said might be interpreted as a bad thing, because this was trigonometry. It wasn't easy material. But his energy seemed to infect the class. And all the time he offered the promise of help. If you can't, we'll all do it.
>
> In a corner of the room was a student named Ben, who'd evidently missed a few classes. "See what you can remember, Ben," the teacher said. Ben was lost. The teacher quickly went to his side: "I'm going to give you a way to get to it." He made a quick suggestion. "How about that?" Ben went back to work. The teacher slipped over to the student next to Ben and glanced at her work. "That's all right!" He went to a third student, then a fourth. Two and a half minutes into the lesson—the length of time it took [a] subpar teacher to turn on the computer—he had already laid out the problem, checked in with nearly every student in the class, and was back at the blackboard to take the lesson a step further.

"In a group like this, the standard MO would be: he's at the board, broadcasting to the kids, and has no idea who knows what he's doing and who doesn't know," Pianta said. "But he's giving individualized feedback. He's off the charts on feedback." Pianta and his team watched in awe. (as cited in Gladwell, 2009, p. 329)

The danger in observing an exemplary teacher is that we can relegate these experiences to the realm of mystery. Why is he such a great teacher? Some people might conclude that it must be a combination of talent, intuition, mystical insight, and a knack—he just "has it" (*it* being those amazing qualities that all exceptional teachers share). However, we might not say that about a great physician, scientist, attorney, race car driver, violinist, or basketball star. Indeed, the overwhelming evidence is that talent is not a mystery but something developed with deliberate practice (Colvin, 2008; Ericsson, Charness, Hoffman, & Feltovich, 2006). Can we apply that generalization to teaching? Here, too, the evidence demonstrates convincingly that feedback, along with other effective teaching techniques, is a skill that can be observed, applied, practiced, and improved (Lemov, 2010).

The Four Elements of Effective Feedback

As we have seen, the clear preponderance of evidence is not only that feedback is important in influencing student achievement but also is relatively more important than almost any other student-based, school-based, or teacher-based variable. It should be noted that evidence on the power of feedback is hardly restricted to the world of education. Dianne Stober and Anthony Grant (2006) and Alan Deutschman (2007) provide evidence from a wide range of environments that depend on feedback, including health care, prisoner rehabilitation, recovery from addiction, and education. Kerry Patterson, Joseph Grenny, David Maxfield, Ron McMillan, and Al Switzler (2008) add to the body of evidence, using cross-cultural examples in which people are engaged in significant and profound change, even though they cannot read or write.

In brief, it is not the provision of a data-driven, decision-making seminar that helps individuals, organizations, or communities change.

Instead, it is the ability to use feedback in clear and consistent ways. However, even the most clear and vivid feedback is useless if not applied with the FAST elements. Each of these is a necessary but insufficient condition for improvement. If information is accurate but not timely, it is unlikely to lead to any improvements. An autopsy, for example, is a marvelously accurate piece of diagnostic work, but it never restores the patient to health.

Almost every teacher I know labors to be fair, excluding any bias regarding gender or ethnicity, in their evaluations of student work, but the pursuit of fairness can impair accuracy. This is particularly true when teachers conflate a student's attitude and behavior with the quality of his or her work. Many computer programs can provide rapid feedback, but if that feedback only informs students whether their performance is correct or incorrect, they will gain little information about how to improve the thinking process that led to an incorrect response or how to sustain the analyses that led to a correct one. Specificity is a component of effective feedback, but reams of data delivered months after students leave school are as ineffective as the detailed criticisms written on the high school English paper mailed to the student weeks after final grades are assigned.

Let's take a closer look at how each of these FAST elements relates to feedback.

Fairness

My favorite lesson in fairness came from Mr. Freeman French, my junior high school orchestra conductor, who had students audition from behind a curtain. Neither students nor the teacher knew the gender, identity, ethnicity, or socioeconomic status of the player. We could only hear the music. While Mr. French's commitment to fairness may seem extreme, it represents a commitment to principle that seems elusive in the context of bias that ranges from Olympic skating to World Cup soccer in which, to put it mildly, fairness is not always the primary value on display. Certainly the blind audition approach of Mr. French had its limits—he ultimately had to look at his performers and give them feedback face to face, but the tone of fairness that he set in his classes conveyed the fact, as well as the impression, that our screeching strings—sharp and flat, too fast or too slow—elicited his feedback solely based on our work and not our appearance.

I am certain that the vast majority of teachers aspire to be fair, but the distortions in feedback based on gender, ethnicity, and socioeconomic status are too consistent and too vast to be explained by performance alone. Similarly, the relationship between socioeconomic and ethnic variables and student test scores is consistent and pervasive (Putnam, 2015; Herrnstein & Murray, 1994), but those relationships say more about how popular tests value what wealthy white students know than they do about the intellectual incapacity of poverty-stricken minority students.

Unfortunately, the cure for unfairness in standardized tests can be worse than the disease, if teachers seek to compensate for unfairness by awarding high grades for poor performance. The pursuit of fairness at the expense of accuracy and specificity does not advance the cause of equity.

Accuracy

We would all like to think that our feedback is accurate. After all, people with college and graduate degrees know more than their students, so their feedback has to be accurate, doesn't it? In fact, it would be more precise to say that our advanced education has provided us with specific knowledge, while feedback must be an accurate reflection of what a student has learned or not yet learned. Factual accuracy and contextual accuracy are the first two principles of accurate feedback. The distinction between factual and contextual accuracy not only is important for classroom teachers but also for school leaders and policymakers. The third principle of accurate feedback is questioning. Asking students questions, rather than just making factually accurate statements, leads to a deeper understanding of students' thought processes.

Factual Accuracy

When teaching single-digit addition to first-grade students, the statement "No, Timmy, two plus three is not four; two plus three equals five" is factually accurate. However, before we take that for granted, it is worth recalling that many highly regarded tests fail even this basic requirement. Almost every year, clever students find that there are either no correct answers or more than one correct answer on high-stakes college admissions examinations. Moreover, student writing is now required on the SAT, the Graduate Record Examinations (GRE), the Law School Admission Test (LSAT), and the Graduate Management Admission Test (GMAT), just to name a few exams with profound career and financial consequences for test takers. While great care is taken to provide consistency between two independent scorers or, in some cases, computerized scorers, this level of accuracy is short of being mathematical. According to a mathematical standard, two plus three equals five all the time, while the statement that an essay is worth 4.5 on a six-point scale is true only to the extent that other scorers agree with the judgment.

This is not meant to suggest that performance assessments, including work involving student writing, speaking, experimentation, and demonstration, are necessarily so subjective that they should not be used. Rather, an appropriate modesty about our professional practices requires that we check the accuracy of our feedback on performance assessments, just as we check the accuracy on a test of single-digit addition. While we cannot have perfect accuracy, we can have a level that is sufficient to lead students to improved performance.

This leads to the first principle of accurate feedback: a variety of observers, including other teachers, student peers, and the students themselves, must understand the criteria the teacher uses. In the previous example, how would you react if a teacher walked into the room and said, "Timmy, if you think that two plus three equals four, then that's fine with me, because the most important thing for me is that you love school!" Some readers would, of course, suggest that loving school and having mathematical accuracy are not incompatible. In fact, we would express concern that if students do not learn number operations through a steady diet of feedback, correction, and improved performance, the chance that they will love future schooling in mathematics is very low.

If we are going to require consistent feedback based on well-understood criteria, we should expect the same of every aspect of feedback, including those areas commonly thought to be subjective.

Students who receive feedback on a writing assessment know little about the criteria if they only can say, "I got a 2 on my paper." Another student, using the same scoring rubric, might be able to say: "I got a 2 on my paper because I left out the three supporting details I was supposed to put in the second paragraph. Also, my introduction didn't tell the reader very much about what I was going to write about. When my friend Laura read it, she said I should use more power words like *awful* or *horrible* instead of just writing *bad*. I think next time I can get a 3 if I work harder."

Note that this is not a problem of specificity—both students have the same rubric. Indeed, in many classrooms, rubrics overwhelm students. The problem is a fundamental issue of accuracy—if a student does not know what the rubric means, he or she cannot assess its accuracy. Just as a student can know that two plus three equals five and not four by engaging in experiments, so can a student understand that rich details, compelling introductions, and vivid language make for improved writing. Knowledge is not just the result of the teacher making pronouncements of judgment but of students understanding these judgments.

Contextual Accuracy

Let's return to the original feedback from Timmy's teacher. "Two plus three is not four," said the teacher, with unassailable accuracy. However, while no one would contest the next statement, "Remember, two plus three equals five," it does not necessarily meet the standard of contextual accuracy. Contextual accuracy requires that feedback reflect the context of what the student has and has not learned. In this example, how would we respond if the teacher said, "No, Timmy, two plus three is not four, and remember that standard deviation is the square root of the variance"? The expectation that first graders are able to grasp statistical functions is silly and irrelevant to the lesson. In the same way, we cannot provide feedback that accurately reflects what Timmy has learned and not yet learned until we do some further inquiry.

Questioning

Questioning as a means to provide accurate feedback is hardly new, as Socrates demonstrated more than two millennia ago. Sometimes it can lead a student to identify a thought process: "Why do you think that is true?" At other times, questions can help a student use another process to test his or her thinking: "What would the answer be if you used the blocks to find it rather than a pencil and paper?" Similarly, on writing and performance assessments, feedback that consists only of teacher statements (such as "Unclear sentence," "Awkward construction," "Improper usage," and "Another grammatical mistake") fails the standard of contextual accuracy.

For some students, these statements are as impenetrable as a gymnastics score during the Olympics. It's a mystery to me, but perhaps it's absolutely clear to an avid viewer of gymnastics competitions. Similarly, members of Garrison Keillor's mythical Professional Organization of English Majors (POEM) may be able to decipher what *awkward construction* means, but most of my students (including more than a few English majors) need some dialogue to sort it out. "Could you please help me better understand this sentence?" can help students distinguish clarity from opacity and replace an awkward expression with one that is more graceful.

While these examples apply to classroom interactions between students and teachers, the principles supporting accurate feedback apply in every context, including feedback provided to teachers and administrators. Whether in the form of annual test results, classroom observations, or formal evaluations, feedback does not meet the fundamental standard of accuracy if the criteria for evaluation are not understood clearly or if they are applied inconsistently.

When I discuss with teachers and administrators the value of feedback, they might respond with a weary, "We've already done that," referring to improved practices with rubrics, collaborative scoring, or student conferences. However, if I turn the tables and ask about their experiences when on the receiving end of feedback, they quickly dissect the inaccuracies and inconsistencies of the evaluations they received. "I'm the same teacher today as I was last year, yet depending on who is making the observation, I'm either superior or in need of improvement. It's a crazy, unfair, and wildly inaccurate system!" So it is, and one of the central purposes of this book is to ensure that we provide students with feedback that is at least as accurate as we provide for the adults in the system.

Specificity

The third element of effective feedback is specificity. Feedback must be specific. There is a long-running dispute among assessment writers about the use of different kinds of rubrics and the relative merits of holistic and analytic rubrics. Grant Wiggins (1998) explains that a holistic rubric "yields a single score based on an overall impression" (p. 164). By contrast, an analytic rubric "isolates each major trait into a separate rubric with its own criteria" (p. 164). The essential principle, however, is not the label of the rubric but the degree to which it is applied consistently. Therefore, when we use rubrics that contain terms like *little evidence* followed by *some evidence*, *sufficient evidence*, and *superior evidence*, we are inviting chaotic ambiguity.

The antidote to ambiguity is not micromanagement. Students, administrators, and teachers have all uttered those words, signaling the surrender of independent thought ("Just tell me what to do") when ambiguous directions frustrate them. Hard work and collaborative efforts, when accompanied by failures in mindreading, can lead to disappointing results.

Certainly, hyperexplicit instruction is tempting. When we are specific with our requirements, students, teachers, and leaders may do exactly what is required, neither more nor less. Students produce essays with precisely five paragraphs, never more parsimoniously or extravagantly detailed than the formula suggests. Teachers print lesson plans precisely as prescribed and write state standards and learning objectives on the board. School administrators create strategic plans that conform to the format and style that higher authorities require. However, when feedback is too specific, students are assessed only on the extent to which they can follow a formula, not engage in learning. Telltale signs that well-intended rubrics have been subverted into mindless formulas include student work that almost uniformly begins with the same sentence.

How can teachers reach a balance between feedback that is too specific and feedback that is too ambiguous? Two principles, pulling in different directions, help teachers strive for this balance. The first involves boundaries and our interpretations of them, and the second involves consistency.

Boundaries

There are one hundred yards from one end of a football field to the other, not including the two end zones, and each team is allowed to place eleven players on the field, provided that the players remain on their own side of an imaginary line—the line of scrimmage. These boundaries are explicit and unchanging. The decision about where to place the players within them, however, is a judgment call. Similarly, fixed boundaries for classroom feedback include spelling and mathematical accuracy, but whether *egregious* should be substituted for *terrible* or whether bar charts should be oriented vertically or horizontally is a judgment call.

For five years, I served as the volunteer coach of a local high school debate team. Students have explicit boundaries, including time limits for speeches, the resolution that they must debate, and the integrity of the evidence they use during the competition. This experience serves as a useful illustration for the essential balance between explicit and flexible feedback on student performance. Applying excessively rigid boundaries for students may unintentionally lead them to become parrots instead of debaters, mimicking the arguments and evidence that they find on commercial websites that cater to affluent schools and students. Thus, the judges of these unfortunate students listen to the same speeches, arguments, and even grammatical errors, round after round, tournament after tournament. The students read the computer printouts, with their intensity interrupted only by the sound of the timer indicating that their time has expired.

If their competitors are locked into the same trap of specificity, then they might not refute their opponents' arguments but instead respond with another commercially prepared speech. These exchanges are not illuminating for the judges, competitors, or audience; therefore, these debates represent the opposite of the critical thinking and rhetorical engagement that the activity might have offered to them.

An opposite but equally pernicious trend has emerged, which debate theorists label the critique (Hensley & Carlin, 2005). Students argue that debate resolutions are artificial boundaries and they should be free to address issues of greater importance to society. We will overlook, at least in this context, the fact that these students and their coaches embrace, without a hint of irony, rules about time limits, ballots, speaker points, and most especially, trophies. It is not that they truly want the absence of rules but rather they want to select the rules that are most familiar to them and least familiar to their opponent. It is as if one football team rolled onto the field equipped with tanks rather than shoulder pads but insisted that the time limits and boundaries of the playing field remain the same.

Where is the middle ground? In the classroom, as in other endeavors, there is a blend of specificity and creativity. Within a single debate resolution, students can think of hundreds of arguments. Within the rules of football, there are thousands of different offensive and defensive formations. One reason I enjoy watching cricket is the seemingly infinite variety of ways that players can respond to a unique combination of batsman and bowler. There is a balance between boundaries and freedom, and that is not only a key to effective feedback but to surviving in a free society.

Consistency

Expect consistency about boundaries but variations in student performance within them—a direct result of variation in judgment calls. How consistent is good enough? Feedback that is sufficiently specific should be consistent 80 percent or more of the time (Porter & Jelinek, 2011). Why is 80 percent important rather than 50 percent or 90 percent? When psychometricians, experts on measurement and testing in the field of psychology, evaluate high-stakes tests, they use the term *reliability* to assess the test's consistency. They expect students who answer a test item correctly to answer similar items correctly. Reliability is never perfect, but in general, the more consistent a test, the more reliable it is deemed to be. As a practical matter, testing experts generally expect about 80 percent consistency (a reliability coefficient of 0.80) on tests for them to be deemed accept-ably reliable; in other words, independent raters agree at least 80 percent of the time.

Classroom feedback should be similarly consistent. About four out of five teachers who look at a piece of student work should agree that it is proficient or not proficient. The more specific the feedback guidelines, the more consistent—the more reliable—the feedback.

Let's apply this theory in practical terms in the classroom. If five sources—three peers, a teacher, and a student doing a self-assessment—provide feedback on student work, four of those five sources should be consistent. That is, the feedback includes the same score on the rubric and very similar suggestions for improvement. This standard allows for some differences—interpersonal relationships can influ-ence peer feedback, and some students can be hypercritical of their own work. However, if a student is not receiving consistent feedback, then the culprit may well be ambiguous qualifiers, such as *sometimes*, *sufficient*, *adequate*, or *good*, which invite different feedback on the same work.

Timeliness

When we say that feedback is timely, we mean that students receive the feedback with sufficient promptness to influence their performance. For example, in most sports, video games, and music rehearsals, feedback is virtually instantaneous—the bad play, wrong maneuver, or sour note is met with immediate feedback that leads students to stop and improve their performance. When conducting a science lab, solving a complex equation, or writing a paper, however, the length of time separating performance from feedback may be significantly longer.

In the context of student work, the extent to which we meet the standard of timeliness influences when the student can use feed-back (Salem, 2013; Mester, 2011). For example, Lucy Calkins (1983, 1994), founder of the Teachers College Reading and Writing Project at Columbia University, pioneered a process in which students receive feedback from peers, teachers, and systematic self-assessment in order to improve the quality of their writing. Her rich illustrations demonstrate the value of feedback (Calkins, 1983, 1994). The difference between poor writing and great writing (particularly from a gifted learner) is not the student's background or teacher but the quality, consistency, and frequency of feedback. I've watched Professor Calkins present these examples in small seminars and in large audiences of more than two thousand teachers, but despite changes in the learning environment, participating teachers' insight is invariably the same: they can't believe that the different writing examples are from the same students. The students are the same; what changes is the quality of the feedback.

The greater the number of students, the more challenging it is for teachers to provide timely feedback. Accomplishing this in secondary schools, where a teacher may have five different classes with thirty or more students each—more than one hundred fifty in all—is a particular challenge. However, it is not impossible. At Harlem Village Academy Charter School, more than 98 percent of students pass the New York Regents Exam, far above the city average (Harlem Village Academies, 2015). In this school, 100 percent of the student population is from a minority ethnic background and three-fourths are eligible for free or reduced-price lunch, a measure of low family income (U.S. News and World Report, 2015). Students routinely give one another feedback on everything from mathematics problem solving to behavior in the hallways.

Self-assessment also can be a rich source of timely feedback, provided that students are able to engage in an objective comparison of their work to a clear standard. An environment of consistent and timely feedback offers multiple benefits for a school, and it is the opposite of a system in which the only person qualified to provide feedback is the one holding the red pen, the gradebook, or the bullhorn. The essential requirement for timely feedback is that students have multiple sources of information, including a clear and consistent system of peer assessment and self-assessment. While it may take a teacher a day to grade homework and tests, student feedback is immediate, often within minutes of a peer's performance.

While the use of scoring rubrics since the 1990s has certainly been a positive step forward, there is wide variation in the quality, consistency, and clarity of these instruments, particularly if students are to use them quickly and accurately. Larry Ainsworth and Jan Christinson's (1998) *Student-Generated Rubrics* is a useful beginning, but the ultimate test of rubric quality is not the words on the rubric itself but its impact on student work. For example, I have created what I thought were stunningly clear writing rubrics for my students, only to find that in their second drafts, they made the same errors—perhaps a bit more neatly—as they did in their first drafts. In other words, a well-crafted rubric met with students' uncomprehending compliance fails to deliver timely feedback. Therefore, while the expert who crafts a rubric may wish to include many elements, it is necessary to provide just enough feedback at the time it can be used to improve performance.

Effective athletic coaches are masterful at this, as are the most effective orchestral and choral conductors. While ineffective coaches hurl an unending stream of criticism and directions from the sidelines to their bewildered players, the best coaches give direction in a way that influences the action at precisely the right time. Similarly, it is interesting to watch how two of the great symphonic conductors of our time, James Levine and Lorin Maazel, move so little, even during rehearsals. Their feedback is precisely at the point in the music when it has the maximum impact. On the best athletic teams and in symphony orchestras, there is an exquisite network of communication—the alert from a fellow player, the arched bow, the lifted head—all of which reinforce and support feedback from the coach or conductor.

Good performance assessments, like good coaching, provide feedback that is FAST—fair, accurate, specific, and timely. The feedback is fair because it is consistent. Good rubrics provide the same score for the same performance. The feedback is accurate because it assesses precisely what it intends to assess. For example, an accurate assessment of writing considers the student's final draft after several attempts and clear feedback, not the first draft. Feedback is specific—consider the examples of the athletic coach and conductor—because students are able to respond to the feedback and demonstrate improvement. Feedback is timely because, when students have a role in producing rubrics, they can assess their own work immediately and identify the next steps.

Table 3.1 summarizes techniques for ensuring fair, accurate, specific, and timely feedback.

Table 3.1: Elements of Effective Feedback

Elements of Effective Feedback	Techniques for Effective Feedback
Fair	Gender, ethnicity, socioeconomic status, or other characteristics of the students do not influence feedback.
	Teachers do not seek to compensate for biases in other tests by displaying reverse bias or awarding disadvantaged students higher grades for lower performances.
Accurate	Different observers, including other teachers, student peers, and the students themselves, understand the criteria the teacher uses to provide feedback.
	Teachers do not just make factually accurate statements to students; they ask students questions.
Specific	Boundaries are distinguished from judgment calls.
	Feedback on boundaries is consistent, with variations in expressions of student performance expected within those boundaries.
Timely	Feedback is delivered incrementally, at precisely the time when students can use it to improve performance.

In this chapter, we considered the four elements of effective feedback: fairness, accuracy, specificity, and timeliness. The next chapter turns its attention to the specific form of feedback known as grades, beginning with an overview of grading issues and the debate that surrounds them.

Chapter 4

THE GRADING DEBATE

As the preface suggests, establishing areas of common ground should form the beginning of any discussion and debate about grading practices. Sadly, this pursuit of common ground has been lacking in many public discussions and debates.

Starting the Debate: Challenges and Responses

Because the debates about grading policies can be vigorous (and sometimes vitriolic), it is important to identify the challenges and potential responses to critics of grading policies and reforms, as shown in table 4.1 (page 48). It also is important to defuse the debate by identifying what will *not* change. For example, even with standards-based grading systems, students can still have letter grades, grade point averages, transcripts, and academic honors. In this chapter, we consider how to engage in a meaningful debate about grading policies while maintaining a healthy respect for the critics of these policies.

Part of professional responsibility is not merely rendering a judgment but also using inquiry to investigate what works to improve student results and professional practices. A mere concession to the notion that we must all defer to the professionals in charge would stop any professional endeavor in its tracks, because change in any field—such as education, medicine, or engineering—is difficult, and the early adopters of change are rarely popular.

Table 4.1: Challenges and Responses to Grading Policies and Reforms

Challenge	Response
Standards-based grading is just grade inflation—more students get higher grades for completing less work.	This is partly true—more students do get higher grades in a standards-based grading system. That's not because they do less work but because the teacher's response to missing or inadequate work is not a 0. Rather, it requires that students do the work, resubmit it, and respect teacher feedback. That's not grade inflation—that's work inflation. More work equals higher grades.
Standards-based grading gives students credit for work they didn't do. The minimum 50 is the craziest idea education has ever had!	Actually, it's the second craziest idea in education. The prize for first place is the claim that the difference between A, B, C, and D should be ten points—scores of 90, 80, 70, and 60—but the consequence for failing to turn in work is zero points, sixty points lower than a D. Let's throw out the minimum 50 idea, and instead, just go to the old-fashioned system in which A = 4, B = 3, C = 2, D = 1, and F = 0. That's the way grade point averages have been calculated for more than a century—it's hardly a new idea, and it's far more accurate than the one hundred–point scale. By the way, vendors of electronic gradebooks don't run the school system, so they don't have the right to require schools to use antiquated and inaccurate one hundred–point scales and average scores. Schools should insist that technology vendors use a 4, 3, 2, 1, 0 scale for grading and allow teacher judgment, not the arithmetic mean, to determine the final grade.
Standards-based grading means the loss of honor rolls and academic honors.	Schools with standards-based grading can keep their honor rolls and academic honors. Many prestigious high schools and universities confer degrees with highest honors, high honors, and honors. This makes far more sense than the claim that the student who has a 3.998 grade point average is superior to the student with a 3.997 grade point average.

Challenge	Response
Standards-based grading isn't fair to students who complete their work correctly the first time and submit it in a timely manner.	Standards-based grading rewards a good work ethic. That doesn't mean finishing work quickly but rather finishing work—sometimes after several drafts—well. The workplace model of the 21st century is not, "Here's the work—it's not very good, but at least it's on time." Rather, the model in every quality-focused workplace involves work, feedback, and improvement.
Grading-reform policies, especially those that prevent teachers from giving zero points for missing work, infringe on teachers' professional judgment. The argument for professional autonomy is a strong one, linked closely to teachers' legitimate desire for personal respect of the knowledge they have acquired over the years and their detailed understanding of the students they teach. In Edmonton, Canada, a teacher refused to follow the school policy preventing 0s and was suspended. This was followed by a protest with students, parents, and fellow teachers, including a candlelight vigil (Zwaagstra, 2012). Neither the suspension nor the protests were particularly helpful in establishing a tone for rational discourse on the matter.	If teachers want to give zero points in extreme events, such as when students persistently miss work and deadlines, then teachers should have that choice. But it must be mathematically accurate—that is, a 0 on a four-point scale. This way, a single missing assignment influences, but does not dramatically distort, the final grade calculation. To emphasize the mathematical inappropriateness of 0 on a one hundred–point scale, consider the reproducible "Distortions in Grading Through the Use of Zero Points" (page 158). The first number line shows a scale from 0 to 4. The second line shows a scale from 0 to 100. Notice that the space for failing grades—those below a 60—is dramatically greater in the second line than in the first line. The third line illustrates the inappropriate use of a 0 on a one hundred–point scale by placing the 0 precisely where failure—score of 60—lands on the second line. As you move from right to left, you are soon in negative territory. In fact, if you ask teachers what score a student should receive for missing work, they most likely would say, "Zero," certainly not the absurd score of minus six. These three number lines illustrate that 0 on a one hundred–point scale is inaccurate and unfair. It creates a huge zone of failure that cannot be rationally justified. Alternatives to 0s are discussed in chapter 11 (page 121).

I've been to enough parent meetings on this subject to know that mutual respect and understanding work far better than expert pronouncements. Both sides in this debate love students and want the best for them. Let's dial back the rhetorical heat and seek some common ground.

Winning the Grading-Reform Debate

For the most part, the fall welcomes teachers and students who are happy and optimistic, renewing old friendships and making new ones. Whether it's in the weekend and evening Twitter chats between teachers or from parents walking their children to school, there is an undeniable enthusiasm in the air at the beginning of the school year. Until, that is, it's time for the first-term report cards. As surely as the leaves fall from the trees in late autumn, the optimism of the first days of school can evolve into student disappointment and, sometimes, angry confrontations with parents. Each year, teachers and administrators ask, "What happened to all those good feelings?"

Here's what happened: parents, teachers, administrators, and students all saw it coming. Capable students received failing grades because of missing homework; students received unexpectedly good or bad grades (neither of which were motivating), because they could not explain how to avoid low grades or achieve higher ones; parents became frustrated because they thought that "everything was OK" and now find themselves dealing with the humiliation of their children failing to meet teacher expectations. Teachers are frustrated because they handed out their grading policy the first day of school, and every student (and often every parent) signed it. Every year we see this coming, and every year we repeat it. It doesn't have to be this way.

Let's be practical. This book is not about a top-down grading-reform initiative. If you announce a plan to reform the grading system, then you just signed up for an inflexible five-year plan (or more specifically, a planning period that outlasts the contracts of current principals and superintendents). But if you just make a few relatively minor changes, you can dramatically reduce the likelihood of another grading train wreck. Too many grading-reform efforts have failed due to fears that any change in policy is both too easy on students and too oppressive in limiting teachers' professional discretion.

Here's how to make some grading reforms *right now* without subjecting yourself to an acrimonious and fruitless political battle.

State What Will *Not* Change

Reassure stakeholders about what will *not* change. Parents and college admissions offices will still have GPAs—the old-fashioned system of a 4 (A average) to a 0. Students will still receive letter grades. These two concessions bring the forces for and against grading reform much closer. The researchers and scholars cited in this book have been writing about this issue for decades, and I've tried to contribute to this literature as well. They are right on the research, and they are right to be fierce in their advocacy. My suggestions for compromise are not intended to undermine their work but rather to suggest what we can do *right now* to avoid the grading train wreck.

Change the Scale to Match the Grades

Whether you use a handwritten notebook or an electronic grading system, change the scale to match what grades really are— 4 (A average) to 0 (for incorrigibly missing work). At the very least, this avoids the disastrous use of 0 on a one hundred–point scale. Any vendor of an electronic grading system who tells you that this is impossible should be disregarded. It is possible to change the numerical scale from one hundred to zero points to four to zero points—just demand it.

Ask for a Fair Warning Agreement From Teachers

Any prospective grades of F, D, or C should result in a call, email, or note to parents at least two weeks before the end of the grading period as well as a meeting with the instructional team, warning parents and colleagues of the possible grades and specifying what is necessary to improve the results. Even if you have a standards-based grading system, the same fair warning applies to descriptors such as *developing* or *in progress*. Students not only need to know where they stand but also what they need to do in order to improve. Teachers don't want students to fail, and these conversations are much easier to have before grades are delivered than afterward. By the way, even if your report card claims that C is average, it's just not true—check what the average grade really was last year, and more importantly, look at the quality of C work—it's frequently awful and needs to be improved if students are to move on to the next grade level with confidence and success.

Require Consequences for Missing or Inaccurate Student Work

Critics of grading reform love consequences, and many sincerely believe that grading as punishment is successful—never mind decades of work from Guskey (2015) and others to the contrary. But let's change the consequences from Fs and zero points to something much more scary: doing the work. Some schools do this during lunch, others before and after school, and others during prescribed catch-up periods. But in every case, appropriate consequences lead to fewer failures, better behavior, and less stress for teachers, parents, and students (Reeves, 2012b).

I would love to engage in a school, district, and national conversation about improved grading policies. But for right now, I just don't want to see teachers, administrators, parents, and students driven crazy by yet another year of toxic grading policies. These simple ideas can help.

And now, if you're ready for the details of how to make this work and how to make your grading system FAST—fair, accurate, specific, and timely—then please consider the chapters that follow. You will find the latest and best evidence, some surprising ideas, and most importantly, practical steps you can follow to make *immediate improvements* in your grading system and provide evidence of effectiveness this year.

Chapter 5

HOW TO IMPROVE FAIRNESS

Almost everyone wants to be fair, and most of us think that we are fair, particularly when it comes to making decisions about students. The fact that some students do better than others is part of life. There are winners and losers in athletics, mathematics, writing, music, and many other endeavors. The work of K. Anders Ericsson, Neil Charness, Robert Hoffman, and Paul Feltovich (2006), as well as that of Hattie (2009), strongly suggests that deliberate practice is what separates top performers from others. Stanford researcher Carol Dweck (2006) admonishes parents to praise children for their work ethic, not their innate ability, so that young people learn to adopt a mindset that associates growth with hard work. In school, we have honor rolls, valedictorians, and scholarships to honor the efforts of those who work harder than others, or so the theory goes. This chapter explores the hypothesis that academic rewards and punishments are, in fact, bestowed fairly.

What Fairness Really Means

Fairness is not a philosophically elusive concept. Most people, at some point in their lives, have been on a school playground and heard the plaintive wail, "That's not fair!" Perhaps a student received assistance from a classmate in what should have been an individual performance, stepped outside the boundaries of the game, or otherwise flouted the rules that almost all young children engaged in playground activities understand and apply. Children don't mind losing—not nearly as much as their parents do—but they are offended by cheating. On the playground, when students perceive that a game is unfair, they simply stop playing. Fairness is not just about the existence of rules and their careful enforcement.

As we move from the playground to the classroom, fairness means that the evaluation of a student is based on the performance of that student. On the soccer field, it would be unfair (though not out of the realm of possibility) for a parent to leap in front of the goal to prevent an opponent from scoring. What about when a parent helps a child with homework, writes a fabricated excuse for missing work, or appeals to the administration for reconsideration of a low grade? If we accept that fairness means the evaluation of a student is based on that student's performance, then we must also be clear that the evaluation is not a function of any of the following.

- Student work that, in fact, another student performed
- Tools available to one student but not available to other students
- Influence available to one student but not available to other students

The formulation seems reasonable enough, until we consider the real world of the classroom, in which different levels of assistance, tools, and influence are not only common but also intentional. Some of these differences are not the result of parents who are preoccupied with the success of their own children. Students with disabilities, for example, receive assistance that is not available to other students; this includes special education teachers, assistive technology, and teams of advocates. Moreover, great teachers routinely make themselves available to provide additional help to struggling students, and outstanding schools create intervention programs for students who need personal and intentional support to succeed.

Suddenly, the concept of fairness becomes much more problematic. Evaluation is not, it turns out, merely a function of the performance of a single student, because that formulation of fairness depends on an assumption that is deeply flawed—the assumption that all students enter the classroom with equal advantages, equal access to support, and equal backgrounds. Education systems do not provide an environment of fairness when they merely confirm the disparities with which students begin their schooling. The challenge is how to reconcile the need for different levels of support for students with the need to provide grading and feedback that are fair and accurate.

Some schools have attempted to address this challenge by noting on report cards that a grade or evaluation mark was achieved with assistance. This may be a useful indicator, provided schools use it on a consistent and rational basis. If, however, the school uses the *with assistance* notation only for students with special needs who receive assistance from a special education teacher but not for privileged students who surreptitiously receive assistance from parents and tutors, then we have hardly reached any reasonable standard of fairness.

In sum, when we say a grade is fair, what we really mean is that the grade is a reflection of the student's performance as well as the context of that performance. That is why a lone letter or number can rarely provide a fair representation. The grade of B– could mean any of the following.

- Outstanding effort and perseverance, but the student has not yet met grade-level standards
- Outstanding performance well above grade level, but the student's attitude, work ethic, and class participation are inadequate
- Superior performance, except for one incident of cheating that resulted in a score of zero points on a major exam
- Failure to meet all academic standards, but the student earned several extra-credit points to merit the final grade

If you are the college admissions officer looking at a transcript, the parent examining a report card, or the teacher of a new class attempting to learn more about your students, you will see none of these explanations, only the grade of B–. The grade without context is without much meaning. Fairness, it turns out, is a quality that has implications for the student earning the grade as well as for other people who use the information that grade represents.

Why Fairness Matters

When we consider the issue of fairness in school, there is a significant consequence to our efforts. When we succeed at fairness, more students are engaged in the pursuit of academic excellence, and parents, future teachers, colleges, and other stakeholders trust us. When we fail, students withdraw, and we produce cynicism and distrust. The widespread belief that grades are not fair leads, unfortunately, to a greater reliance on simple mathematical formulas that depend solely on standardized tests (Lehrer, 2009). Moreover, when perceptions of unfairness are pervasive, there is a hidden impact on student motivation. Girls are not underrepresented in mathematics and science disciplines because of neurological differences, but because they have received the relentless message, from early adolescence to graduate school, that these disciplines are part of a man's world. When there are enormous imbalances in student success based on gender, the society at large suffers, because half the available brainpower does not attempt to play the game.

The point is not just that we should have more women in mathematics and science but that, as a society, we benefit when we have more people in mathematics and science—and in teaching, art criticism, psychiatry, culinary arts, neurosurgery, or any other field. If we wish to cultivate excellence at the top of any field, then we need more people who are willing to engage in the attempt. Failures at fairness not only limit opportunities for the individual student but also the size of the pool of potentially outstanding performers in every discipline.

Why Social Class Matters

Harvard Professor Robert Putnam (2015) documents the dramatic relationship between social class and educational results. This relationship not only is a consequence of schools in neighborhoods of low socioeconomic status but also the home environment before school even begins. Moreover, Putnam concludes, students who are economically disadvantaged—who are also overwhelmingly ethnic minorities—suffer significantly greater consequences for misbehavior, ranging from class disruptions to serious incidences of drug and alcohol abuse.

One of the most important predictors of success in high school and college is the extent to which students learn to *play school*—that is, they know when to ask for help, who can be reliable sources of assistance, and how to fit in with the prevailing expectations of authority figures.

Orlando Griego (educator and founder of the La Familia Scholars Program) was formerly head of a postsecondary institution in Colorado with the largest ethnic minority population in the western United States. Griego noticed that while young Latinas were enrolling in college in record numbers, they also were failing many classes, particularly in mathematics and science. The numbers were particularly alarming for students who had children. The family, not school, was the center of their lives. Their sense of family obligation was different from that of other students who were young and unmarried. Even for Latina students who were young and single, the responsibility for child care, he found, frequently extended to nieces, nephews, younger siblings, and other members of the extended family. Their role as caregivers was an important part of their identity, and academic success depended on integrating academics within this social structure and not making family alienation the price for achievement (O. Griego, personal communication, January 3, 1994; Roueche, Roueche, & Ely, 2002).

Griego created the La Familia Scholars Program in order to build a family-oriented, supportive environment for Latina students. The students were given their own room for study, food, socializing, and academic support. They were able to find assignments and test dates online and didn't need to explain to the professor why they missed a class to care for a sick child. They were able to learn the fundamentals that their course syllabi assumed they had already mastered. They also were recognized publicly as La Familia Scholars, a term that included the precise blend of their pursuits but also signaled to the family and academic communities the priority that family and scholarship played in their lives.

Griego's efforts paid off, dramatically reducing the Latina dropout rate. More importantly, he provided a model for the entire college system of how a commitment to equity need not compromise academic rigor but must take into account the needs of a diverse student body (O. Griego, personal communication, January 3, 1994).

Why Equity Matters

The reproducible "Equity in Grading Self-Assessment" (page 159 and online at **go.solution-tree.com/assessment**) provides a nonjudgmental guide for teachers and education administrators who are willing to explore the extent to which their grading systems, and the applications of those systems, are fair and equitable. This self-assessment is designed for classroom use, but it can be modified for use by an entire school or school system.

Certainly, it is possible that this exercise reveals nothing of significance and that, in fact, it confirms a high degree of equity in your grading system. However, it also is possible that you will make observations that are comparable to the following, which I have seen when working through these data with teachers.

- Students on the honor roll but with low scores on external tests are more likely to be female; and in urban systems, they tend to be minority females. This observation is consistent with national data that suggest that female students perform markedly better than males in high school and matriculate in college by a significantly higher percentage compared to their male classmates (Kafer, 2005). Females also are significantly overrepresented in academic recognitions that are exclusively reflective of grades.

- Students with low grades and high scores on standardized tests are more likely to be male; and in urban systems, they tend to be minority males. Rebelliousness and defiance among adolescent boys are hardly a news flash, and in the power struggles of middle and high school, one of the few tools available to teachers is the grading system. Boys accumulate Fs and receive zero points even as their analytical ability improves. In fact, punitive grading systems serve as a reward, telling them that "no make-up" rules mean more free time.

The foregoing points may strike you as offensive overgeneralizations, but before you come to that conclusion, consider conducting the following experiment for your school, as I was compelled to do with mine (Reeves, 2006a).

- How many girls were inducted into the National Honor Society last year? How many boys? What is the ratio, and how does that compare to your student population?

- What was the ratio of girls to boys on the honor roll?

- What was the ratio of girls to boys who failed classes?

- What is the gender ratio in remedial courses? What is the ratio in advanced courses?

See if a clear pattern emerges in your school.

Fairness is an essential element of grading, but it is not sufficient to form a fully satisfactory system of student evaluation. Grading systems also must be effective, a complex requirement that includes accurate, specific, and timely feedback on student achievement. The next chapter explores how teachers and school leaders can establish more accurate grading systems.

Chapter 6

HOW TO IMPROVE ACCURACY

In previous chapters, we looked at the grading debate and considered how fairness can affect grading systems. While no grading system is perfect, we can take clear and definitive steps toward improving the processes and practices of grading.

Sometimes, teachers defend the accuracy of a grade because the final result conforms to the mathematical system that they created, but this sort of numerical precision creates only the illusion of accuracy. For example, the use of the arithmetic mean, or average, might be calculated accurately, but however accurate it might be, the use of the average undermines grading accuracy. You would never, for example, decide whether or not to wear a coat on January 31 based on the average temperature during the month. You would want to know the temperature on that day and make your decision accordingly.

This chapter first explores how to measure accuracy and then looks at how to improve it.

Measuring Accuracy

Let's continue the analogy to temperature. Jacqueline B. Clymer and Dylan Wiliam (2007) suggest that we think about the relationship between grades and temperature this way: a thermostat provides information about the current temperature, just as a grade should tell us what a student knows and can do at the moment. A thermostat also gives us a way to set the temperature we would like to have, just as a feedback-oriented grading system clearly shows a standard that students must achieve. This information reveals the difference between where students are now and where they need to be, just as we know that raising the room temperature from fifty to seventy degrees requires more energy than raising the temperature only two degrees. Finally, as in a heating system, where we have a choice of interventions—heat, cold, fan, or nothing—a teacher can decide which strategies to use based on the feedback he or she receives (Clymer & Wiliam, 2007).

Consider how a middle school science teacher might transform this theory into action by creating a system with the following features.

- Assessments are designed to provide feedback—they are not the final grade.

- Grade records are informative, allowing both the student and teacher to understand that different starting points are required for different students.

- Feedback is continuous and flexible. Grades could rise or fall based on student performance.

- Final grades are based on the student's actual work and achievement, not the intelligence, aptitude, and prior knowledge that the student had before the class began.

Students' responses to this system would most likely be overwhelmingly positive. The vast majority of students would understand the fundamental principle of this system—that personal effort and continuous learning are the primary causes of their grades. They also would appreciate the fact that their grades could always be improved. These students would ask more questions, become more involved in their learning, and like the specific and detailed feedback.

Some critics assail case studies and other action research because they lack the elegance of a true experiment, with random assignment of students to control and experimental groups (Campbell & Stanley, 1963). While formal research is important, we should not neglect the value of action research observations such as those from Clymer and Wiliam (2007). In fact, Clymer was able to control experiments far better than many people who completed more formal projects. For his work, we used the same teacher, with the same curriculum, in the same school, and the same or very similar student characteristics before and after the grading experiment. The only major change was the new grading system. Therefore, we can be reasonably confident that it was that change—a consistent, accurate, feedback-oriented grading system—that led to improvements in student performance and engagement.

Thus, we can claim that grades are accurate only when those grades reflect what students know and can do when the grade is awarded. This means that the use of the average is almost always inaccurate, unless student performance oscillates around the mean throughout the year. For the average to accurately represent student performance, student progress would look something like figure 6.1, an unlikely and disappointing experience.

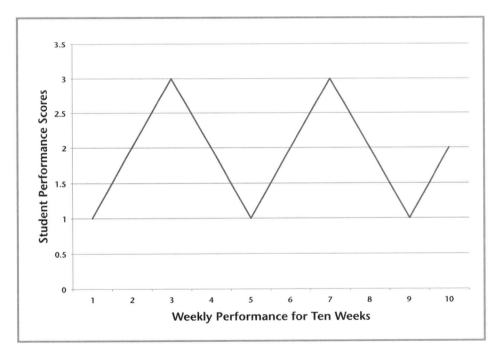

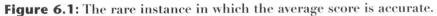

Figure 6.1: The rare instance in which the average score is accurate.

This unfortunate student made progress at first but then dropped back to where he started. Most teachers observing this would intervene, recognizing that something was wrong with the student's performance and engagement, and that perhaps improvements were needed in teaching and feedback. The virtue of this example is that it illustrates the very rare instance in which the arithmetic mean, or average, meets our standard of accuracy, since the grade represents student performance at the end of the marking period. Of course, most student performance is not at all like that depicted in the figure. Student performance is not stagnant; it typically improves over time. Figure 6.2 is far more representative of real student performance, in which students begin slowly, receive feedback, become more motivated and competent, receive more feedback, and ultimately demonstrate gains.

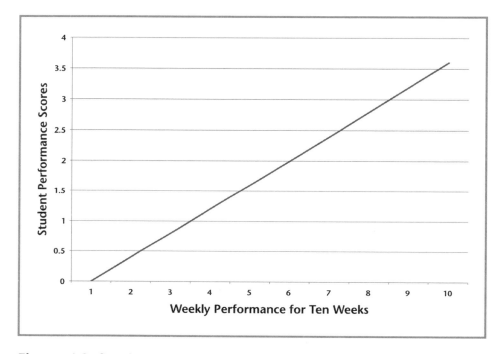

Figure 6.2: Steady progress, the more typical student performance.

Compare the student performances in figures 6.1 and 6.2. Would you agree that they are significantly different? The student represented in figure 6.1 makes fits and starts but never sustains any gains in learning. The student represented in figure 6.2 makes steady progress, ending the year at 3.6, a significant improvement—but this student's average is the same as that of the student in figure 6.1. It would not be accurate to say that both should receive the same grade. Grading systems that use the average—even when they carry out the calculation of the average with great mathematical precision to several decimal places—are wrong. The real life of the classroom is not linear; it involves fits and starts and successes and failures. Some lessons result in "aha" moments, and some leave students bewildered. It still happens to me every week. Almost always, however, by the end of the term, we have made significant progress.

A more accurate description of classroom life is represented in figure 6.3.

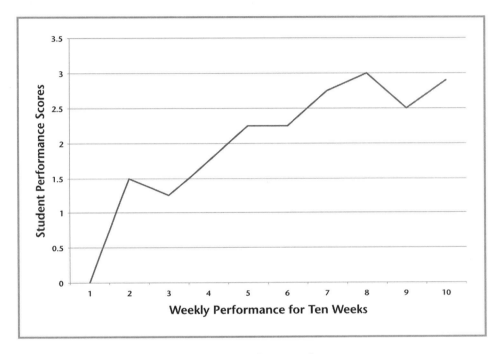

Figure 6.3: Realistic variations in student performance.

These sorts of variations are common, with some weeks punctuated by gains and others by losses; occasionally the performance is level. Sometimes these variations are due to teacher actions, and other times there is social drama, distraction, or encouragement at home; support from peers; technology disasters; or any number of other week-to-week vicissitudes that prevent student performance from achieving the artificial linearity of figure 6.2. However messy the reality of figure 6.3, this student's performance deserves a higher grade than the student performance represented in figure 6.1.

In sum, the use of the average may appear to be precise, but it is not accurate, because it does not meet our standard of accurately reflecting student performance.

How can you assess the accuracy of your grades? Start by working backward—identify students who, at the end of the year, have the same letter grade. I find that this is most effective when you consider students with the grade of B, because it is commonly one of the least accurate grades if the standard of accuracy is a reflection of student performance. Once you assemble a small sample of students with the same final grade, look at their performance. How is it similar? How is it different?

Consider three vignettes of student performance in a secondary school mathematics class. Each of these students received a final grade of B. While the descriptions and names are composites of many students, the reader can judge the extent to which these examples ring true.

Sean

Sean received a B because of his exceptional effort and diligence. He turned in homework every day (though the answers were seldom correct). Each time he received a D or an F on a quiz, he came to class and asked for help, and the teacher worked through the problems with him. Sean also completed a creative extra-credit project, creating a mural with mathematical equations in a caption over one of the people he depicted. Finally, he received citizenship points for his good behavior during class.

Sam

Sam received a B because his surly attitude and rude and disrespectful behavior deserved, in the teacher's opinion, some sort of consequence. It seemed as if his papers, always accurate and submitted on time, had been wadded up deliberately. Sam finished every quiz and test before the rest of the class, and he smirked at his fellow students who still labored to complete their work. But the final straw was when Sam cut several classes. He thought that because he submitted his homework in advance (flawless, as usual), and there were no quizzes or tests on those days, he could get away with it. But the departmental policy is clear—unexcused absences result in zero points for the day, and that brought his A+ performance down to a B. Another colleague who observed the entire affair concurred, saying, "The jerk got what he deserved."

> ## Maryellen
>
> Maryellen was an average student. She did most of her homework, received Cs and Bs on her quizzes, and with some extra credit, was able to get a C+ on the final exam. She never gave the teacher any trouble, and her parents were strong and vocal supporters of the school. With a little extra credit, Maryellen, too, received a final grade of B.

When the same grade is associated with wildly different levels of performance, the grading system is inaccurate. The same technique—working backward from a grade to examine the relationship between the grade and student performance—also can be used with individual pieces of student work. In an experiment with fifty classroom educators (Reeves, 2006a), I provided an example of student work that had been awarded a B and then removed the grade and any identifying information that would reveal the name of the student, teacher, or school involved. I then asked these teachers to assign their own grade to the work. In twelve different work samples, I found that the grades from other teachers varied widely. Guskey and Bailey (2001) come to similar conclusions, noting that it does not matter whether the grading system is subjective, such as grades associated with student writing, or objective, such as grades commonly associated with mathematics. All the grades were subjective, because the same performance resulted in different grades.

Improving Accuracy

Although every endeavor involving human judgment is subject to error, we can nevertheless make efforts to identify, quantify, and reduce these errors. For teachers, this is a continuous process, and we never achieve an error-free state of perfection. We can, however, make significant improvements in grading accuracy through frequently using reality checks, utilizing collaborative scoring, and avoiding unintentional mathematical distortions in our grading policies.

Reality Checks

The two essential reality checks for grading are the comparison of student results to external measurements and determining whether students are receiving behavioral grades.

External Measurements

For some classes, the learning objectives are closely aligned to external assessments. Examples of this close alignment would be courses that are associated with advanced placement (AP), International Baccalaureate, Cambridge International Examinations (CIE), or other standard assessments that are directly linked to class curriculum. In these cases, a high score in the class should be strongly associated with high scores on the external exams. When there is a divergence, only a few explanations are possible. If the external exam results are lower than the classroom scores, we might conclude that the student just had a bad day or that the items on the test were unusually difficult.

However, if this happens with more than a few students, two other explanations are more likely. First, the taught curriculum and the tested curriculum are not aligned. This is particularly likely to happen when teachers are unfamiliar with the external examination or if they retain a strong affinity for their previously used curriculum. In these cases, the tested curriculum is treated as an extra burden rather than the academic core of the class. By contrast, teachers who are deeply familiar with the external examination—particularly those teachers who have served as official examiners for the testing organization and read hundreds of examinations from students in other schools—have an exceptional advantage. They not only know their subjects, but they also know how students are evaluated. The closer the relationship between classroom teaching and external assessment, the lower the chance for error due to misalignment.

Behavioral Grades

The second and more common cause of divergence between grades and external results is the conflation of academic performance and behavior. When grades are high and external results are low, we should ask how much of the academic grade is, in fact, a behavioral grade. For instance, some students may be rewarded for quiet and compliant behavior and receive higher grades than what they would receive strictly academically. Conversely, when grades are low and external results are high, we should consider the possibility that the low grades are a reflection of behavior that displeased the teacher. In both cases, these are grave inaccuracies in grading. The error is not in the attempt by teachers to encourage good behavior. The error is the mislabeling of behavior as *algebra* or *chemistry* or *history*. If we wish to address student behavior in an effective manner, then let us call it what it is.

Of course, for most teachers, there is no convenient external exam, such as AP or CIE, to serve as a reality check for a comparison of classroom grades and academic success. However, many other sources of information can help focus grades on academic performance and reduce the probability of inaccuracy. The use of academic performance scoring rubrics, for example, allows teachers to focus exclusively on the knowledge and skills of the student. Our rubrics might reference, for example, the design of experiments that test a hypothesis, rather than state that the student will test the hypothesis with a cheerful and compliant disposition.

Collaborative Scoring

Perhaps one of the best and most practical ways to improve accuracy is to collaboratively score student work. This is also a superb professional learning experience, allowing teachers to improve the quality, consistency, and timeliness of their feedback to students. Sometimes, collaborative scoring occurs informally, as when a teacher asks a colleague for help: "I'm on the fence about this particular project—how would you evaluate it?"

However, the most effective collaborative scoring processes I have observed follow a consistent protocol in which the identities of the students and teachers are unknown to the teachers who are scoring. The only question is, "Given this particular piece of student work and the scoring rubric I have available, what is my assessment of the work?" Accuracy not only improves because practice with a rubric leads to consistency but also because teachers have constructive discussions about their disagreements. This leads to improvement in the clarity and specificity of the scoring rubric. Figure 6.4 (page 70) illustrates improvements over time with the same teachers engaging in collaborative scoring of student work. The vertical axis represents the percentage of agreement among teachers, and the bars represent the first, second, third, and fourth practice sessions.

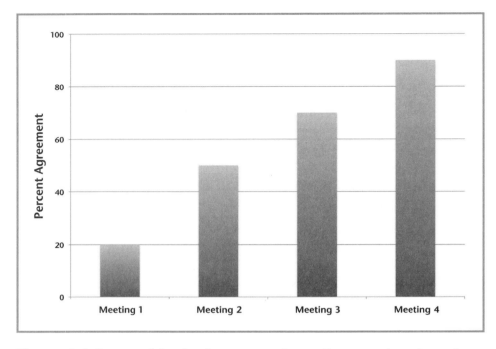

Figure 6.4: Improved levels of agreement in grading over time through collaboration.

Finally, the use of collaborative scoring techniques gives students feedback that is timely. This is because teachers use scoring rubrics more frequently, and as they refine the clarity and specificity of those rubrics, they are able to evaluate complex assessments more quickly. Figure 6.5 demonstrates the impact of consistent practice on the speed of grading. The vertical axis represents the minutes required to score an assignment, and the bars represent—once again—the first, second, third, and fourth practice sessions. With practice, accuracy improves and so does timeliness. Ask yourself when you last had a professional learning experience that both improved the quality of instruction in a key area—feedback—and also saved time for teachers.

Unintentional Mathematical Distortions

The last practical method for improving accuracy involves avoiding unintentional mathematical errors. Earlier, we addressed how the 0 on a one hundred–point scale creates mathematical distortion. Some schools use the minimum 50 policy to avoid this distortion.

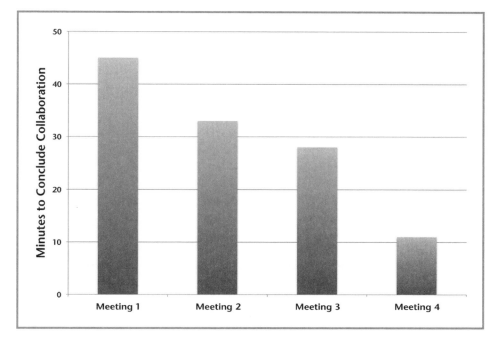

Figure 6.5: Improved speed of collaborative grading over time.

Unfortunately, this leads to a good deal of political discontent, because it appears to critics that students are given fifty points without doing any work. Therefore, if it is psychologically necessary for stakeholders in your area to have the 0 as an option for teachers, then we can remove its mathematically distorting impact by using a four-point scale rather than a one hundred–point scale. This may require some adjustments to electronic grading systems, but it is not impossible. If teachers wish to preserve the fine distinctions among students that the one hundred–point scale creates so they can distinguish between the bragging rights of students with an 85.6 instead of an 84.3, then the same precision can be used with the four-point scale by allowing several places to the right of the decimal point. However, when a 0 is used, it cannot, by definition, have an impact any greater than one point below the D, which is worth one point.

The other source of mathematical distortion, as we learned at the beginning of this chapter, is the average, or arithmetic mean. The best alternatives to the average are the use of accumulating points or the ability of the teacher to weight end-of-year assignments much higher than early assignments. This would work the same way that track coaches consider times at the end of the season more relevant than those at the beginning. Similarly, when students are creating computer programs, their work is not judged on the average number of errors in the program during the semester but on the quality of their programs at the end of the year.

The same is true in art and music—and there is no reason that this sort of thoughtful judgment cannot be applied in every academic subject. Electronic grading systems that default to the average are simply wrong, and teachers must have the ability to override their mindless calculations in order to substitute a superior grading policy that links student grades to student performance when those grades are awarded rather than at the end of the year.

No matter how accurate grades are, however, they will not be credible with stakeholders if they are not specific. The next chapter explores the third element of grading—specificity.

Chapter 7

HOW TO IMPROVE SPECIFICITY

Although specificity is a key to improved grading practices, most grading systems engage in the strange practice of reducing a complex set of variables into a single letter or number. Grading should be designed to improve communication, making clear to students, fellow teachers, and future teachers the student's academic performance. Effective communication is impossible, however, if the people involved do not know or agree on the relationship between performance and the numeric or letter symbols that appear in grades. If a student receives feedback on his or her performance written in ancient Egyptian hieroglyphs, then no matter how well intentioned the teacher who provides the feedback, it is unlikely he or she would learn much from the exchange.

The work and thought put into most grading systems are impressive; many teachers invest a lot of time in their grading systems. Unfortunately, they often seek to provide a rationale that makes sense to the system's designer and administrator. However, the rationale is sometimes without communicative value to students, parents, fellow teachers, and other school systems that may want to evaluate transcripts in the future.

One of the principal controversies in grading is the extent to which grading should be limited to students' demonstration of academic ability and the degree to which it should reflect a range of other characteristics, including work habits and personal character.

Ken O'Connor (2009) is a leading advocate of the principle that "effort, participation, attitude, and other behaviors shall not be included in grades" (p. 250). Critics often respond, "But don't you care about attendance, attitude, and behavior? In the real world, our graduates are evaluated based on these matters every day!" A careful reading of O'Connor (2009) reveals that he cares very much about these matters. He cares so much about effort, participation, attitude, and behavior that he suggests teachers label these variables *effort*, *participation*, *attitude*, and *behavior*, not *mathematics*, *English*, *history*, and *science*. It is precisely because these and other characteristics are important that we should improve the specificity of grading.

Gauging Knowledge

The best way to grade what a student knows and is able to do is to report specific student performance relative to an objective standard. Many kindergarten report cards do this with clarity and precision, specifying, for example, the numbers and letters a student knows. Physical fitness and music tests also tend toward this degree of clarity, communicating the number of exercises that a student can perform or the key signatures of the scales and arpeggios that a young musician can play. We can, if we choose, do the same in other subjects, using tools such as the standards achievement report.

However, teachers need not use the standards achievement report *in place of* a traditional letter grade. Secondary schools, in particular, feel compelled to use letter grades to produce a transcript, and cultural imperatives in many education systems make the designation of a letter grade essential. Therefore, the argument in favor of improving specificity is not about eliminating letter grades; it is a suggestion to communicate them in a manner that is clearer and more meaningful for students, parents, and fellow teachers.

Translating Standards Into Grades

How do we translate standards achievement into grades? One simple system considers a combination of student performance and ultimate performance during a term. Suppose there are six assessments during a term. An assessment could be a research paper, an in-class test, a lab, a demonstration, or other significant evidence of student learning. In figure 7.1 (page 76), we will assume that each assessment is evaluated on the following four-point scale.

4 = Exemplary

3 = Proficient

2 = Progressing but not yet proficient—more work is required

1 = Not meeting standards—the student requires intensive intervention and extensive work in order to make progress

As these labels suggest, the scores 4, 3, 2, and 1 do not nearly translate into the letter grades A, B, C, and D, because a grade of C typically qualifies a student for work at the next level. In this standards-based system, however, a score of 2 is not proficient work. The labels also imply that each assessment's evaluations are not designed as a final determinant of student ability but rather as feedback to improve learning. The score of 2 does not mean "You didn't do very well, but move on to the next assignment anyway." Rather, scores of 1 and 2 explicitly require additional work. Nevertheless, there comes a time when grades are due, so how can teachers communicate both a clear record of student progress and a letter grade? Following is one system to consider.

A = At least four assessments with a final score of 4 and two assessments with a final score of at least 3

B = At least four assessments with a final score of at least 3 and two assessments with a final score of at least 2

C = At least three assessments with a final score of at least 3

Feedback and Improvement

Let us stop and consider the important implications of this system so far. First, the use of the term *final score* suggests that students submit their work, get feedback, and improve. The A student, therefore, is not necessarily the one who receives a score of 4 on the first submission of every assignment but rather the student who

Washington High School
Standards Achievement Report 2001–2002

Student Name: _____

Class: _____*Biology*_____   Teacher: _____

E = Exemplary (4); **P** = Proficient (3); **IP** = In Progress (2);
N = Not Meeting Standards (1)

Assignment	Standard						
	Biodiversity	Genetics	Cell Structure	Environmental Interrelationships	Explanation of Scientific Conclusions	Teamwork	Submission of Work on Time
Lab 1	P (3)			P (3)	P (3)	E (4)	N (1)
Analytical paper 1	P (3)				P (3)		IP (2)
Lab 2	P (3)				P (3)	E (4)	IP (2)
Analytical paper 2		P (3)			P (3)		IP (2)
Lab 3			E (4)		E (4)	E (4)	N (1)
Analytical paper 3			E (4)		E (4)		IP (2)
Synthesis 1	P (3)	E (4)	E (4)		E (4)		IP (2)
Lab 4				P (3)	P (3)	E (4)	IP (2)
Analytical paper 4				P (3)		P (3)	IP (2)
Lab 5		P (3)		P (3)	P (3)	E (4)	N (1)
Analytical paper 5		E (4)		E (4)	E (4)		IP (2)
Lab 6				P (3)	E (4)	E (4)	P (3)
Analytical paper 6				E (4)	E (4)	E (4)	P (3)
Synthesis 2	E (4)	E (4)	E (4)	P (3)	E (4)		P (3)

Note: *Not every assignment encompasses every standard, but every assignment addresses several of the most important standards for this class. Moreover, the teacher clearly identifies that there are both academic and behavioral standards for students. This particular report is the profile of a student who is proficient or exemplary in every academic standard but displays a rather consistent inability to turn in work on time. The feedback this report displays is far more revealing than a letter grade.*

Figure 7.1: Sample standards achievement report.

uses the teacher's feedback, works harder, and ultimately receives the better evaluation. This strategy encourages work ethic, respect, and determination. Dweck (2006) and Angela L. Duckworth, Christopher Peterson, Michael Matthews, and Dennis Kelly (2007) contribute landmark research to the field, indicating that these characteristics—what Duckworth calls *grit*—are among the most important not only for student success but also for later academic and work success.

Quality, Not Just Quantity

A second implication of this system is that teachers emphasize quality rather than quantity in student work. While the grade of C typically is associated with work of poor quality, in this system, the grade of C requires that students submit—and most probably resubmit—work that meets the standards of proficiency established for the class. However, the C students complete only three of the assessments at this level of quality. These students are not rewarded for a large quantity of low-quality work, since they are asked to focus on meeting the requirements for proficiency. In other words, if a student submits three pieces of work three times—a total of nine submissions—this leads to a higher level of quality, because the student is incorporating teacher feedback and improving along the way. This is ultimately better than a student who submits nine pieces of work one time but never uses teacher feedback to improve performance. In simple terms, a C student in a typical class receives a C for poor work, while a C student in this class completes fewer assignments but of higher quality.

The Coward's F

A third implication of this system is that there is no D, a grade I have described as the *coward's F*. When the possibility of a D is part of a grading system, it legitimizes the worst of all possible worlds, in which students can pass a class and proceed to the next level of instruction with the virtually certain prospect of failure. Worse yet, the availability of a D encourages the least-motivated student to do the least possible amount of work. While some teachers use the D as a punishment for poor work and inadequate motivation, the D is, in fact, a reward for bad behavior. It tells the student, "You really don't have to listen to the teacher, resubmit the assignment, or redo the work. Just do enough papers, quickly and badly, and we'll let you skate through to the next grade."

Listening to Students

In order to determine whether or not this grading system is appropriate for students in your school, you might consider doing what I did—ask the students. If you decide to do this, it is important to provide a confidential and anonymous environment. For example, the faculties of two schools might want to agree to a reciprocal action research project, in which the teacher researchers of Washington School interview the students at Jefferson School and vice versa. I have been fortunate enough to conduct personal interviews and focus groups with many students on this subject, asking them about which grading systems lead to higher levels of achievement. Students respond to my questions with astonishing insight. One secondary school student, whose anonymity I guaranteed, said this regarding the previously described grading system:

> I hate it. Last year, you could do anything and get a D, but now you have to work really hard to get even a C. In fact, it's such a hassle to get a C, you might as well get a B. (Personal communication, January 10, 2002)

In the spring of 2005, I interviewed more than ninety secondary school teachers and parents on the subject of resubmitting work. The responses were interesting. While there was initial resistance to the idea of anything except punishment for poor or missing work, teachers came to realize that the consequence for students of doing the assignment at a proficient level was far more meaningful than simply receiving a low grade. Parents, who often expect teachers to be the enforcers of good student work ethic, also came to understand that students getting work done, even after multiple attempts, was a more meaningful way to build work ethic than the tradition of low grades as punishment.

When students receive explicit and specific feedback on their performance and are required to submit work, they are not happy about it, but they nevertheless perform at a higher level. For many teachers—particularly those whose job security is sometimes related to their degree of popularity with students and parents—this conclusion presents a difficult dilemma. "To what extent can I risk making students mad?" they wonder. "What if I am effective as a teacher but unpopular with my students?"

The value of specificity applies not only to student performance but also to teacher quality (Corbalan, Plaza, Hervas, Zaragoza, & Arcega, 2013). The landmark work of Oxford researcher Herbert Marsh (1984) supports this concept. Marsh is the creator of the Students' Evaluation of Educational Quality (SEEQ) instrument and a prolific researcher and writer. With more than one million administrations of the SEEQ, the instrument's reliability and validity have been established by independent scholars from around the world. Marsh documents what most parents and teachers—particularly parents and teachers of adolescents—know to be true: students crave challenges. While they rarely appreciate it in the moment, they admire most teachers who demand their best. Conversely, students disdain patronizing, ridiculing teachers who think that the way to the students' hearts and minds is through low expectations.

My extensive correspondence, received both personally and vicariously through the blogosphere, suggests that many defenders of traditional grading systems believe the "real world" does not allow multiple opportunities for success. "You know it, or you don't" is a common refrain, as is "In the real world, you've got to get it right the first time." This hypothesis can be tested at once. Select some people you respect—physicians, scientists, electricians, pilots, architects, engineers, attorneys, diplomats, plumbers, teachers, or mechanics— and then pose this question: "Is the model of professional success that has served you best one that insists on a one-shot performance with success on the first attempt, or is your model of success based on trying it, getting feedback, and improving it; trying it again, getting feedback, and improving it again?"

The stakes could not be higher, whether it is the engineer and architect who design the skyscraper or the electrician who must depend on his or her calculations while balanced precariously in the air. The appellate attorney in a capital case bears a heavy responsibility, as does the teacher who either nurtures the abilities of his or her students or alienates them from learning. What do the best of the best in these professions really do in the real world? As a rash of research suggests (Colvin, 2008; Ericsson et al., 2006; Gladwell, 2008; Hattie, 2009), expertise is not developed based on the mystical ability of professionals to get it right the first time. Rather, it is based on the willingness to try techniques; get feedback that is fair, accurate, specific, and timely; and then improve performance.

Considering Thinking Processes

Some student discussions about grading tend to be binary ("I got the grade I wanted") or attributed to forces beyond their control ("The teacher didn't like me"). On the other hand, academic discussions of grading and student performance can be mind-numbingly abstract, with long forms containing terms (*phonemic awareness* and *metacognition* to name a couple) that are alien to many students and parents. However, several researchers have brought clarity and specificity to this otherwise difficult subject. An important example of presenting ideas about student learning and recognition of their success, along with complex thinking processes, is Stanley Pogrow's (2009) explanations of higher-order thinking skills.

An ardent and thoughtful advocate of HOTS—higher-order thinking skills, Pogrow has enlightened an entire generation regarding the value of appropriate complexity in the classroom. The challenge that vexes teachers (and more than a few parents) is how we distinguish students' thinking from the decisions they make. In an algebra problem, this question is of only abstract interest, but in the decision making of teens about drugs, alcohol, and sexual behaviors, it literally can be a matter of life or death. Therefore, it is a matter of more than passing interest that we consider it.

For many students, there is a clear but unstated equivalence between *smart* and *fast*—that is, the really smart student is not the one who discerns the meaning of *eudemonic* from its cognate roots but rather the student who memorizes it from a spelling list or a video from *The Onion*. In fact, the ability to reflect on our thinking processes is more important than always having the right answer, no matter how quickly we arrive at it or how accurate it may be. In their landmark research on the subject, W. Chan Kim and Renée

Mauborgne (2003) and their colleagues at INSEAD, one of the world's largest graduate business schools, learned that decision-making processes are more important than the decisions themselves. This is strikingly counterintuitive, particularly for Americans, who claim to be bottom-line oriented. Our rhetoric prefers action and conclusion, but our actual behavior suggests that process is essential, not results alone. Kim and Mauborgne (2003) find that when people disagree with a decision but understand the process that led to it, they are more satisfied than if they agree with the decision but find the process mysterious and unfair.

Collaboration, for example, is a desirable 21st century skill. We should consider which grading practices most encourage this trait. Do these practices reward only the student who is smart, fast, and competitive, or do they encourage the student who is deliberate, overtly thoughtful, and collaborative?

Early in the 21st century, the world endured a global economic calamity in which an exclusive focus on the bottom line, the next quarter's earnings, and the immediately apparent performance led to the exclusion of a thoughtful review of process. We have traversed this territory before. For six years before its collapse in 2001, Enron made the list of the "world's most admired companies" and was hailed as an icon of innovation (Stein, 2000). Fannie Mae was similarly the subject of adulation. Both are bankrupt. Would it have been overly tedious for someone to ask, "We see that the conclusions you have reached are doubtlessly brilliant and that you reached them quickly, but can you say *how* you reached them?" The principle of specificity requires that we not only look at results, whether they are financial or academic, but also how those results were achieved.

In an era of rewards bestowed on students who memorize quickly and test well, we would do well to examine this same question. The point is not to embarrass our best students but to give them what they need most—challenge, engagement, and respect. With declining budgets for assessments, more schools and institutions of higher learning rely on tests that are cheap and worth the price. It falls to teachers and local education leaders, therefore, to ask, "Can you explain how you reached those conclusions?"

Effectively Modifying Behavior

Specificity requires that we clearly distinguish between student academic performance and behavior. For example, one student might receive a C because of poor performance, a cheerful attitude, and diligent work, while another student might receive the same grade as the result of excellent performance but a sour disposition and indifferent work.

We want people to behave better, whether they are the whiny adolescent in our mathematics class, the screaming baby in the grocery store, the ill-tempered businessperson in front of us at the airport security line, or the impatient driver behind us in traffic. In the context of the classroom and the workplace, one of the most common methods to cope with bad behavior is criticism. We'd like to say, "Whining, screaming, huffing, and honking are all ill-considered strategies" or something like that. Criticizing others' behavior certainly feels good, but just like the pigeon leaving a "deposit" on the statue of Lord Nelson in Trafalgar Square, our criticism probably has little impact on the target.

Consider just a few of the student behaviors that many teachers wish to modify—inattentiveness, tardiness, incomplete work, and disrespect. One possible strategy to deal with these behaviors is to shout "Math: B–!" or "History: C!" In this particular strategy, the link made between behavior and consequence leads directly to the student who responds to the parental query, "How did you get that grade?" with the predictable response, "I dunno."

There is a better way. If we would like students to change their behavior, the first thing we must do is identify with precision the behavior we wish to change and then decide, as Michael Fullan (2008b) suggests, if the impending battle over behavioral modification is worth fighting for. If the answer is *yes*, then by all means, let us fight, but let us do so in a manner that has at least some probability of victory. If the school were ablaze and we needed to evacuate the building, no sentient teacher would be shouting "Math: B–!" He or she would instead be giving directions to secure students' safety. Therefore, if inattentiveness, tardiness, and disrespect are opponents worth engaging, what are the most effective methods to do so?

Defining Behavior With Clarity

First, define the behavior with absolute clarity. If, in the context of school behavior, we wish for students to be attentive, punctual, and respectful, then do we assess only their absences, tardiness, and disciplinary records, or do we explore the causes for success and failure in each of these domains? If tardiness is associated with an alcoholic parent who cannot wake up in time to transport a student to school, then a lecture on the value of punctuality is unlikely to be of much help. On the other hand, the opportunity to make up work during structured time in the day may be useful.

With an opportunity for structured make-up work, the student, therefore, cannot use the home environment as an excuse for poor performance, but neither is the home environment an academic death sentence. By defining the behavior, in this case, we indicate to the student that the essential issue is not complying with a school schedule that is incompatible with parental alcohol abuse; rather, the essential issue is getting student work done in a timely and diligent manner.

Similarly, I wish I could say that all of my students walk in the door with the tip of the hat offered to Mr. Chips, the endearing English schoolmaster. The truth is, they don't. Some are invested in the latest app on their smartphones, others are focused on their friends, and others are lost in their own thoughts and preoccupations that I can scarcely understand. There is, however, a middle ground between a contemptuous adjudication of their behavior as disrespectful and the conclusion that they are just kids and, therefore, incapable of giving their respectful attention.

Respectful attention, particularly to adult instruction, is a skill to be practiced. Even the most disrespectful students can learn to be attentive when the object of their focus is a video game or app. What does the video game or app provide to the disengaged student? It provides immediate feedback and guidance and incremental opportunities for improvement. If we wish to improve student behavior, then the pledge to give them a final failing grade and the exchange of contemptuous glances until, mercifully for both parties, the semester ends, is an unlikely prescription for success. Teachers can improve student behavior by considering the lessons of electronic games—using feedback that is immediate, specific, and incremental.

As in the case of academic performance, a rubric might be useful, creating a four-point spectrum of performance. For example, teachers wishing to improve levels of student attentiveness might consider some specific opportunities for improvement along a continuum such as the following.

1. You are asleep, distracted, conversing with others, playing with your smartphone, or otherwise disengaged from the class. You are showing me that you do not even care about the class, your fellow students, or me as a professional educator.

2. You are pretending to pay attention, but we both know it is only superficial engagement. You look forward and have your book open, but you are not participating actively in individual and group work.

3. You are seated when the bell rings and have your book and papers ready. You volunteer to participate in class and group activities. You ask questions and contribute actively to class discussions.

4. You take an active leadership role in the class, noticing when other students need help and encouragement. You regard it as a personal mission to help other students move to higher levels of engagement that you know lead to more success for the entire class.

In sum, effective feedback in grading practices requires specificity. If behavior is important, then our grading practices should label it *behavior* and not *math* or *history*. Our first obligation as teachers and leaders is to describe with clarity and specificity the behavior we wish to achieve. Rewards and punishments are insufficient, as discussed in the next few paragraphs. We must know what we want and describe it with precision.

Using Incentives Correctly

There is rich psychological literature about the relative impact of rewards and punishments. As Daniel Pink (2009) and Alfie Kohn

(1999) document, rewards can be misused. Rewards render students dependent on them and create what cognitive psychologist Daniel Willingham (2009) calls *praise junkies*, students who are nearly unable to engage in work without another jolt of the "praise drug" to their system.

Punishments can be even worse, encouraging students to avoid difficult tasks or modify troublesome behaviors. Students witness the futility of punishment on a regular basis when teachers insist on using grading policies that institutionalize punishment for previous bad behavior. When teachers use the average and zero points, for example, the inattention, tardiness, incomplete work, and disrespect from January is punished well into May. If the same teacher departs from an otherwise strict diet with a donut and ice cream binge on New Year's but resumes his regimen in February, March, April, and May, what matters most is the physical health of the teacher in May. No physician or trainer would say, "I'd give you a clean bill of health and encourage your progress, but I just can't get over that weekend you failed to follow your instructions." If that were the case, we would never engage in the effort to be healthy, emulating the futility and resentment of students who ask, "What does it matter? I can't win. There's nothing I can do. I might as well give up."

Incentive systems, therefore, must provide balanced measures of reinforcement, correction, forgiveness, and resilience. While we must identify and confront poor performance, let us call it what it is—poor performance, not an immutable character flaw. When we want students to pay attention, we can help them practice the essential skill of focus (Gallagher, 2009), but we need not assume that inattention is due to their contempt for our favorite subject. It is also possible that disengagement is related to disappointment over a relationship, their parents' divorce, the death of a loved one, or another cause that, had it occurred in the life of an adult friend, would be perfectly understandable.

Rewards and punishments, when administered with absolute consistency, help a lab rat find its way through a maze. But when these rewards and punishments are administered in a haphazard manner, they drive the same lab rats insane (Lehrer, 2009). In fact, the frustrated lab animal would rather starve to death than pursue a reward that is easily accessible if that reward appears to be inconsistent and unfair, accessible one moment and beyond reach the next.

When it comes to students, we cannot improve behavior with a simple combination of rewards and punishments. High and low grades, honor rolls, detentions, and the host of other recognitions and humiliations regularly used in schools are of little value unless the incentives they seek to provide are clear to students. Ironically, even the best incentive systems sometimes lead to cynicism rather than commitment, an attitude diametrically opposed to what teachers attempt to instill in students.

Encouraging Integrity

No one doubts the need for encouraging academic integrity in our students. The question is what to do about it. Specificity in grading suggests that when breaches of integrity take place, we are precise in labeling the behavior. If we mean plagiarism or dishonesty or theft, then these are very serious allegations that should be called what they are. The more precise our use of language, the more likely we are to help students understand what academic integrity really is.

From 1992 to 2012, student cheating dramatically increased (Perez-Pena, 2012). This not only is the result of efforts by schools to catch students cheating but also the willful and acknowledged behavior of students. Cheating has been widely tolerated, with neither parents nor schools seeming to take the matter very seriously. If we are to restore academic integrity, teachers must have candid conversations about the meaning of cheating. Before we administer severe consequences for breaches of academic honesty, we must first make it clear to students why plagiarism and other forms of academic dishonesty are wrong.

As an illustration, following is a conversation I had with a student I caught plagiarizing red-handed.

"I'd like to have your locker combination," I said in terse but measured tones.

"Why?" the student asked, responsive but not submissive.

"Because," I replied with honest intensity, "I would like to steal your stuff. I'd like to take your smartphone, skateboard, pictures, books, and anything else I want."

After a pause, during which the student had to choose between the absurdity of my demand and the seriousness of my demeanor, she finally asked, "Why? Why do you want my stuff?"

"Because," I said, "you thought it was OK to steal from someone else, so I thought you wouldn't mind if I stole some of your stuff."

"I didn't ever steal anybody's stuff," she responded defensively. "That's not right, and you have bad information. I never steal."

I then presented her paper to her. It was the text of a four-minute speech, which was, word for word, copied from a popular student website to which I subscribe and for which I pay an annual fee. Next to her paper, I provided my download from the site. "Of course you steal," I said. "These words are not your words. You stole them."

This is not a morality tale that has a happily-ever-after ending. The student was indignant. She believed with sincerity that she had done nothing wrong. She was an honor roll student, normally immune from and indifferent to the criticism of faculty members. She had school figured out and understood what she had to do in order to earn good grades, avoid uncomfortable confrontations, and get out of her small town. One thing she had to do in order to earn good grades was copy others' work. It was hardly a moral dilemma. Her older siblings copied music every day from the Internet, explaining that only suckers paid for music and that iTunes was for fools. Her parents sang in a church choir, following carefully the score emblazoned with a watermark the length of the page that read *Do Not Copy*, while the director apparently reasoned that violation of copyright law in service of a deity was acceptable.

What about my student? If she were the daughter of the school board chair, her violation might be viewed as a youthful mistake. If she were the child of an unemployed single mother, her breach of integrity could lead to a course failure, expulsion, and a mark on her transcript that would label her forever as a failure and a cheat.

What if this student were your child? Surely you would not condone plagiarism, but neither would you expect that she should receive academic corporal punishment for her bad judgment. You might even acknowledge that you, as a parent, had some role in her flawed decision making. Remember, this student did not fail to turn in work, the consequence for which is almost always zero points. She did not turn in the work late, the consequence for which is frequently at least a reduction in the final score by one grade. She did not fail to work—she actually worked very hard, scanning several websites to find the perfect place to copy, cheat, and plagiarize her way into the honor roll. There are several alternatives to consider.

The first and most commonly used consequence is reward. That's right—we talk a good game about academic integrity, but we routinely reward plagiarism. In one case of blatant plagiarism, the punishment was a reduction in the grade from A to B, and even this consequence was greeted with protest from the student and parents. Another consequence is academic capital punishment, including expulsion, transcript notices, or other marks of iniquity that might as well be a scarlet letter on the forehead of the offender. Perhaps a better consequence is the invasion of the locker, a consequence that contemporary students understand: "I will ransack your music downloads, I will tear up your boyfriend's letter, and I will destroy your diary." These are, to most teenagers, far more serious consequences than suspension, expulsion, or reductions in letter grades.

My students are good kids who have a decent moral compass, but most have reached their late teenage years without a clue as to what plagiarism is, without a sense of what integrity means, and without a well-developed notion of empathy. When I tell them, "If you steal words, it's the same as if I take stuff out of your locker," there is a long pause, and the lights go on.

The goal in this chapter was to improve the specificity of grading. If we wish to improve academic performance, attitude, integrity, or any other element of performance, we must be clear and specific about our expectations. The next chapter explores the final element of effective grading practices—timeliness.

Chapter 8

HOW TO IMPROVE TIMELINESS

Feedback, when it is fair, accurate, specific, and timely, has a profound impact on student achievement. In fact, as we have seen, quality feedback can have a greater influence on student results than family and socioeconomic factors. Because grades are among the most essential feedback that students receive, it is particularly important that students receive information about their academic performance in a timely manner. In this chapter, we explore how educators can improve the speed with which they provide feedback to students.

Jeff Howard is the founder of the Efficacy Institute, an organization with a more than two-decade track record of dramatic improvements in the performance of high-poverty urban schools. Howard (personal communication, May 5, 2010) wondered how urban students could be several years behind their peers in proficiency in reading and mathematics yet able to master very quickly the complex knowledge and skills required to obliterate space aliens from a computer screen. The ability to become masters of the virtual universe, Howard observed, was not a matter of blasting away mindlessly at an imaginary enemy. There were a complicated series of moves, often with multiple steps and complex contingencies, which players had to use in order to succeed, in the parlance of gamers, at the "next level" of competition. It just didn't make sense, he concluded, that students could do ten-step problem solving with an electronic game but were judged to be incapable of solving two-step equations in middle school.

The lessons that Howard learned and applied successfully in some of the United States' most challenging schools are the focus of this chapter. Howard called his insight the *Nintendo Effect*, referring to the dramatic improvement in performance that students are capable of demonstrating when they receive immediate feedback and when they have an opportunity to use that feedback to improve their performance.

Why Timely Feedback Is Important

The television drama *Grey's Anatomy* is engaging because, typically, the physicians learn the elusive diagnosis just in time to save the patient. There is drama because the patient might die, and the fiction is credible because many viewers have had experiences, or know of friends or family members with experiences, that resonate with each episode's plot.

"I had symptoms that I thought indicated one diagnosis, but it was something else. I was not a hypochondriac after all but had a real disease. Take that," we say to the doubting family member, friend, or colleague. "I was not slacking; I was really sick. I might have died! Thank goodness for those skilled physicians at Grey-Sloan Memorial!"

The real world, it turns out, has some eerie similarities to this television series, both in the close calls in which timely feedback is necessary to save lives and in the catastrophic consequences that ensue when feedback, however technologically sophisticated and expert, is too late to be of value. Atul Gawande (2009), author of *The Checklist Manifesto*, also leads the World Health Organization's Safe Surgery Saves Lives program and was awarded the MacArthur Fellowship in 2006.

With certifiable genius and advanced expertise in an exceptionally technical field, Gawande might be expected to offer complex solutions to the complex challenges of surgery and critical care in the 21st century. What he provides instead is bound to disappoint those who are held in thrall by the mystery of expertise. Gawande, who is a real genius and does not just play one on television, offers only a boring checklist. His prospects for starring on a television series may be limited, but one thing is certain: he has saved more lives in one week than those doctors at Grey-Sloan Memorial will in their careers, and his insights will continue to do so.

Gawande's secret is the absence of secrecy. By demystifying medical treatment and showing, with overwhelming evidence, that even extensively trained experts would have superior results if they used checklists, he has helped to reduce hospital death rates, frequency of infection, and length of stays in the intensive care unit by orders of magnitude that, as we will see, have staggering implications. Gawande explains that the consequence of violating a checklist is immediate and timely intervention. Surgeons do not receive an end-of-year performance review if they fail to wear a mask when examining a wound. Another member of the team takes immediate and certain action to prevent a patient's infection. The timeliness of this action is essential.

How are classroom teachers like surgeons? Both see a variety of new and unexpected complications every day. Both deal with factors—nutrition, parental behavior, sleep, just to name a few—that can ameliorate or aggravate the conditions of their patients or students, as the case may be, and both have little or no control over those factors. The breadth and depth of complexity in both cases are stunning. Gawande (2009) explains:

> A study of forty-one thousand trauma patients in the state of Pennsylvania—just trauma patients—found that they had 1,224 different injury-related diagnoses in 32,261 unique combinations. That's like having 32,261 kinds of airplanes to land. Mapping out the proper steps for every case is not possible, and physicians have been skeptical that a piece of paper with a bunch of little boxes would improve matters. (p. 35)

A teacher, particularly in a highly complex school with a transient student population in which students speak dozens of different languages at home, suffer from scores of psychological and physiological afflictions, and span perhaps six different grade levels of performance when they enter the classroom, might describe Gawande's dilemma as a normal day's work. Teachers, like surgeons, resist and resent the idea that their complex tasks can be systematized. It is, they argue, more art than science, and those who craft checklists are more apt to give advice than take it. I share this belief, but occasionally my cynicism must give way to the evidence.

Following are a few of the findings in Gawande's (2009) exploration of the virtues of checklists in the medical context.

- Reduced line-infection rates from 11 percent to zero

- Prevented forty-three infections and eight deaths and saved two million dollars in costs—all in a single hospital

- Reduced from 41 percent to 3 percent the likelihood of a patient's enduring untreated pain

- Reduced the proportion of patients not receiving the recommended care by a quarter; twenty-one fewer patients died than in the previous year

- Improved the consistency of care to the point that the average length of patient stay in intensive care dropped by half (p. 39)

The results are not perfect. Doctors still make mistakes, and patients still die. But feedback—particularly when it is provided in a timely manner—reduces the impact of those mistakes in a substantial way. How can we apply this to schools? First, we must acknowledge that the standard for consideration of improved practice is not perfection but improvement. I have presented evidence of how improved feedback policies can, for example, improve homework compliance, reduce unexcused absences, and decrease the failure rate (Reeves, 2009b). Surprisingly, a frequent response to these findings is not, "Thanks, that will make next year a lot better," but rather, "You haven't seen my students—I know of some kids who just never do the work, never show up, and never respond to feedback."

Accepting, for the sake of argument, that these unnamed students are doomed, resistant to any intervention the teacher might offer, their existence should not prevent us from pursuing the greatest improvement for the greatest number of students. The fact that some patients die of infection despite our best efforts does not relieve physicians from the burden of washing their hands, sanitizing the operating arena, and covering their mouths with a surgical mask. If we can ask people with a dozen years of postgraduate medical training to use checklists in order to gain immediate feedback on their practice and make appropriate midcourse corrections, then we can and must ask teachers and school administrators to do the same.

Standards of Timeliness

How timely must our feedback be? In the case of the hospital emergency room, timeliness is measured in seconds and minutes. In the case of playing a video game, the feedback loop is even shorter. What about the feedback for teachers, education leaders, and students? In most school systems, the most important feedback—the data that lead to evaluation, reward, and sanctions for teachers and administrators, and which may determine opportunities for students—is separated from the performance by months. Teachers are routinely summoned to data-analysis meetings in which they are required to analyze data on students who are no longer in their classroom. *Grey's Anatomy*'s audience would surely decline if the physicians descended into a Kafkaesque world in which each episode was an exploration of the maladies of the patient who was featured in the previous week's story—especially if the patient had already died.

Fortunately, we have standards of timeliness that are accessible to almost every school. Just as an emergency room seeks to assess 100 percent of patients in a timely manner and provide care that is appropriate to their needs, so too can a classroom teacher seek to meet the same standard. For example, watch a great music teacher in action—within minutes, the chorus, band, or orchestra is ready to perform, and the teacher is providing feedback to each student on how to improve. Watch a great athletic coach—students do not wait for instruction but take to the field, floor, or ice, shooting baskets, practicing shots, and receiving feedback from both coaches and other students. Can this be applied to the classroom?

At schools around the world, students and teachers use *The Art of Teaching Writing* (Calkins, 1994). Calkins helps students provide feedback to one another, so that every few minutes of every class, students write, read the writing of their fellow students, and give and receive feedback.

When I taught graduate courses in assessment and research, I took my students on a field trip to watch a school basketball game coached by Craig Ross. My students recorded the following observations.

- The percentage of players who received feedback
- The frequency of feedback for each player
- The nature of the feedback—such as negative, positive, prescriptive, or challenging
- The impact of the feedback—that is, did the feedback lead to improved performance?

The results were not particularly remarkable, at least in the context of a basketball game.

- **How many players received feedback?** One hundred percent of the players received feedback.

- **What was the frequency of feedback?** Within a single fifteen-minute quarter, each player typically received feedback between five and fifteen times, the variation depending on the player's needs.

- **What was the nature of the feedback?** The nature of the feedback varied widely. The coach knew that some students needed constant reinforcement, others needed to be challenged, others needed to be reminded specifically of what to do, and others needed to be asked to think about how to respond to a particular challenge. The coach (now the very successful chief executive officer of a global corporation) seemed to understand that different students needed different kinds of feedback, although I'm certain that he never breathed the words *differentiated instruction*.

- **What was the impact of the feedback?** The impact of the feedback was clear—this was a small school with no scholarships, and no one enrolled there because of the basketball program. Yet we beat teams that were bigger, stronger, taller, and better. Our teacher—our coach— never yelled, cursed, or labeled his students, but he gave them feedback that led directly to improved performance.

I then challenged my students to make the same observations in a class at school. The contrast was striking.

- **How many students received feedback?** Typically, there was positive feedback for the eager few who raised their hands and volunteered and negative feedback for the other extreme, the few students who were disruptive. For the vast quiet middle, there was little or no feedback, as if we had made a bargain with them—"Don't bother the teacher, and the teacher won't bother you."

- **What was the frequency of feedback?** It was, in the terms of our research class, a skewed distribution, with most feedback going to a few students.

- **What was the nature of the feedback?** It was almost entirely binary—great/awful, wonderful/wretched, right/wrong.

- **What was the impact of the feedback?** It was difficult to tell, because there was no scorekeeping in evidence aside from the teacher's invisible good and bad marks and the inevitability of a report card nine weeks hence.

In every one of the foregoing examples, the feedback was effective not only because it was specific, but also because it was timely. The students knew immediately how to improve their performance. Ross was an excellent coach and teacher, but his techniques did not need to be exceptional. Providing feedback in every class—even in every "quarter" of every class—is not an impossible standard. Providing feedback that is specific and differentiated and that influences student results is a realistic expectation. We only need to take mathematics, science, social studies, English, and every other discipline as seriously as we take basketball.

How Teachers Can Improve Timeliness

Teachers can accelerate the pace of feedback to students in three ways: (1) involving students in establishing academic criteria, (2) using a three-column rubric, and (3) offering midcourse corrections.

Involve Students in Establishing Academic Criteria

The fastest feedback a teacher can possibly provide to a student is feedback that takes place before the teacher ever even sees the work product. How can that happen?

In *Student-Generated Rubrics*, Ainsworth and Christinson (1998) demonstrate the advantages in terms of clarity and timeliness that occur when students have a hand in creating and applying scoring rubrics in the classroom. Involving students in the creation of criteria for academic performance can be threatening to some teachers; after all, we are the teachers, and our expertise is obviously greater than our students'. While that assumption is generally true, we might be surprised at the level of sophistication and clarity with which students are able to define different levels of performance in an academic context.

Listen, for example, when students explain the rules of a game on the playground: "You can go *here*, but you can't go *there*." "You can do *this*, but you can't do *that*; but if you see someone else do *this*, then you get to do *that*." It's a whole series of complex and conditional rules. The same is true of the precision with which students are able to describe how to do everything from play a video game to survive in the social network of middle school. Once they know the rules of the game, they can evaluate their own performance and that of others, and they can improve at a rapid pace. If they don't know the rules of the game, or if the rules of the game are subject to sudden and unannounced changes (middle school social networks again come to mind), then we sadly observe the result: students simply stop playing the game.

So it is with academic work. Once a student concludes that "I'm just not a good writer" or "I'll never get mathematics," then it becomes strikingly more difficult to restore that student's confidence. Such students have a fixed mindset (Dweck, 2006). They have become dependent on teachers' feedback to affirm their performance, because they have not developed the ability to accurately assess their own work. The result, even among high-achieving students, can be very damaging.

University of Virginia psychological researcher Daniel Willingham (2009) warns of the perils of praise when students crave the adulation of teachers more than the satisfaction of having done a task well. Thus, scoring rubrics that teachers create and apply with students not only save time and accelerate feedback but also build students' analytical insight and confidence.

Use a Three-Column Rubric

The second way for teachers to improve timeliness is with a three-column rubric, with one column for performance criteria, a second column for student self-assessment, and a third for teacher assessment. In many more advanced tasks, student-generated rubrics may not be appropriate, as the teacher must use experience, judgment, and expertise to create them. Nevertheless, we can express the performance criteria in language that a vast majority of students can use. To use the three-column rubric, the teacher creates the first column of criteria in advance of the work, and the student completes the second column before the work is submitted. The teacher, then, need only focus on the third column—those specific performance criteria for which the teacher's performance assessment differs from the student's.

This technique avoids the repetition of obvious corrections and, most importantly, removes the teacher from serving in the factory foreman role, in which the student is the benighted laborer, unaware of the quality of the work he or she has done without the manager's inspection. When the teacher provides feedback only on those areas in which his or her assessment varies from the student's self-assessment, he or she is able to differentiate feedback for each student explicitly, according to the student's needs. Moreover, the teacher is providing fewer comments for each student and focusing them in areas that have the greatest impact on student performance.

I have used this technique with students ranging from primary grades to graduate school, and I have found that it saves hours every week compared to my previous technique of providing laborious written feedback on every assignment. Much like the checklists that Gawande (2009) finds useful in a variety of settings, the student's self-assessment provides a shortcut that avoids a great deal of the mechanical and low-level feedback from teacher to student. Figure 8.1 (page 98) shows an example of a three-column rubric.

Scoring Guide	Student Assessment	Teacher Assessment
1. Organization	1.1 My outline includes two levels of structure, including Roman numerals and letters. 1.2 My outline matches the content of my written and oral presentation. 1.3 My outline follows a logical progression, with facts to support my arguments.	1.3 I don't understand why global warming leads to famine in Africa—could you please elaborate on this?
2. Research	2.1 I have both primary and secondary sources. 2.2 All of my sources are listed in the references. 2.3 My references include citations from both the Internet and books or periodicals.	
3. Written Arguments	3.1 My written presentation follows the outline structure. 3.2 Each sentence is complete, grammatically correct, and every word is spelled correctly. 3.3 Each section of my paper flows logically to the next, and every paragraph has a logical transition to the next paragraph.	3.2 Your writing is excellent! Please see the places where I circled incomplete sentences, and rewrite them for the final draft. 3.3 Please reword the last sentence in the middle paragraph of page 3—I don't understand how it leads to the next section.
4. Graphics	4.1 I have at least three graphs, charts, or figures to illustrate my main points. 4.2 Each graph is explained in the text.	
5. Oral Presentation	5.1 My presentation opens with a compelling story, statistic, or question. 5.2 My presentation explains the ideas in my paper in a clear and logical way. 5.3 My presentation closes with a provocative question or statement that makes my listeners want to learn more.	5.1 VERY interesting—you hooked me! 5.3 I understand your conclusion, but why should I learn more?

Figure 8.1: Sample three-column scoring rubric.

Offer Midcourse Corrections

The third way for teachers to improve the timeliness of feedback is to create midcourse corrections for students before a project's completion. This is particularly useful in major tasks, such as an elementary or secondary school research project. One of the least efficient work processes in schools is the simultaneous submission of major projects on the same day to a teacher who, even with heroic efforts devoting nights and weekends to grading, returns the projects weeks after the students submit them. While I deeply respect the time and attention that teachers devote to evaluating and commenting on these projects, there is one unequivocal rule of feedback that applies here: if students do not ever read the feedback, there is no chance that they will use it to improve performance. Teachers resent the workload, parents complain about dilatory grading, and students consign last week's work to the same brain region occupied by the Ice Age—they are vaguely aware of it, but it has little relevance to their academic life.

There has to be a better way. Midcourse corrections allow teachers to provide differentiated feedback from the beginning of an assignment to the end, identifying and highlighting problems before they begin. A major project might take place over six weeks, which is thirty classroom days on a regular schedule or fifteen classroom days on a block schedule. By allocating ten minutes for two individual check-ins in a regular class of fifty minutes (or twenty minutes for four check-ins during a ninety-minute block), the teacher can create sixty individualized opportunities for review and feedback before the project is due.

Some students might require more frequent progress checks than others. Figure 8.2 (pages 100–101) illustrates how a teacher might provide weekly feedback for students whose history suggests that they need particular help in organization and time management and less frequent feedback to other students. Note that this structured intermediate feedback differs significantly from the well-intentioned offer to "come see me whenever you need help." In fact, students who most need help do not routinely ask for it. Intervention and assistance must be structured. If we expect students to learn the critical school survival skill of seeking assistance and getting timely feedback, then we must teach it to them. Teachers are busy.

Day	Students	Sample Comments
Monday	1, 2	1—Outline not started; 2—Topic not selected
Tuesday	3, 4	3—Lost rubric; 4—Loves topic but overwhelmed
Wednesday	5, 6	5—Needs focus; 6—Detailed outline; ready to go
Thursday	10, 11	10—Very advanced; needs challenge beyond "4"
Friday	12, 13	13—Potentially inappropriate topic; check with parents
Monday	1, 2	1—Outline incomplete; 2—Topic too general
Tuesday	3, 4	3—Folder set up, ready to start; 4—Has good focus
Wednesday	5, 7	5—Clear question; needs step-by-step help
Thursday	14, 15	14—Needs help on primary/secondary source difference
Friday	16, 17	17—Ahead of schedule; completely self-directed
Monday	1, 2	1—Wants new topic—no—complete commitment
Tuesday	3, 4	4—Worked through small steps; much better
Wednesday	5, 8	5—Wants to do personal interviews; excellent
Thursday	18, 19	18—Potential plagiarism; warning and explanation
Friday	20, 21	21—Hasn't started; parents divorcing, needs counseling
Monday	1, 2	1—Changed his mind; loves the topic, has first draft!
Tuesday	3, 4	3—Working the checklist; may not finish on time
Wednesday	5, 9	5—Field notes are a mess; needs organizational system
Thursday	22, 23	23—Exceptional work; almost done
Friday	24, 25	25—Unfocused; did paper before outline; refocus now!
Monday	1, 2	2—Good focus; first draft needs work
Tuesday	3, 4	3—Coordinated with social studies; same topic for both classes; loves the idea
Wednesday	5, 9	5—Organized notes into categories; must write draft
Thursday	26, 27	27—Wants to have web-based appendix; OK
Friday	28, 29	29—Created interactive game; I need to learn more

Day	Students	Sample Comments
Monday	1, 2	1—Needs at least one more draft but will finish
Tuesday	3, 4	3—Rough but is going to make it
Wednesday	5, 9	5—Draft is on Hunter S. Thompson; needs coherence
Thursday	30, 31	31—Thoughtful, challenging work
Friday	32, 33	33—OK; just going through the motions, not to capacity

Figure 8.2: Differentiated feedback for a major six-week project.

With class sizes increasing and the burdens for coverage expanding, even while school days are shrinking, it is difficult to imagine devoting time to individual students. Yet it can be done. Students 1, 2, 3, 4, and 5 in figure 8.2 receive more frequent feedback than their peers, and the comments in the right-hand column suggest why. These students are disorganized, unfocused, and resistant to completing the assignment. More timely feedback—ten minutes per period is devoted to differentiated feedback—does not transform these students into paragons of organization and scholarship, but it does allow student and teacher to collaborate in a way that averts the disaster and failure so often associated with long-term projects. By the time students, parents, and teachers know that there is a problem, it is too late to correct it. Differentiated feedback, by contrast, provides students with midcourse corrections and opportunities for the teacher to intervene where appropriate.

How School Administrators Can Improve Timeliness

Many schools are using what they call *formative assessments* that may or may not be worthy of the name. As W. J. Popham (2008) and Robert Marzano (2009) remind us, assessments are not formative because of the label, but because teachers use them to inform instruction. Different schools in the same system might be using the same assessments, labeled formative, benchmark, or interim, but the interpretation and application of those assessment results depend largely on the way in which the school administration creates time for teachers.

In one school, time is allocated for administration of the assessment, after which teachers sigh, "Thank goodness that's over—now we can get back to what we were doing." The results, if they are transmitted to teachers at all, arrive weeks later after teachers and students have already moved on to new units of study.

In another school, administrators are aware of the need for the application of formative assessment data and allocate time and resources for the analysis and application of such data, as well as for professional learning. Teachers in this school have an intellectual understanding of the value of formative assessment and data analysis, but in the context of a formal class, it remains an abstract notion.

In a third school, however, formative assessment and data analysis are at the heart of weekly professional learning community (PLC) meetings. "It's just the way we do business," explains Superintendent Sandra Thorstenson in Whittier, California (personal communication, August 5, 2009):

> Even if the district takes weeks to give us the final analysis, we keep copies of the formative assessments and evaluate them collaboratively, and students have feedback the very next day on where they did well and how they can improve. As a staff, we know immediately what worked and what didn't, and the exact steps we need to take to be better teachers and leaders.

Although education leaders sometimes bewail their lack of influence on what happens inside the classroom, there is a great deal that they can do to influence in profound ways the timely use of feedback for improving student results.

Consider Practical Trade-Offs

School leaders should consider some practical trade-offs in making the commitment to timely feedback. Their first obligation is to ensure that assessments are focused and brief. School leaders hear a different view from assessment experts, who say that in order to sample a content domain adequately, a test should include five or six items per content area. This is a reasonable statement if the purpose of the test is to determine with statistical precision the student's knowledge about a specific academic content area. However, the practical impact of this standard is that assessments include fifty to sixty items for ten or twelve content areas, and the test may therefore require up to two hours of class time.

Assessments must also be administered within a reasonable period of time—twenty to thirty minutes—and the feedback to students and teachers must be immediate, within one or two days. The best practices I have observed involve scoring periodic assessments the same day, so teachers have the results, analyzed by subject area and student, immediately enabling teachers and students to apply feedback on performance the next day.

The practical realities of education leadership are that we must make choices. We simply cannot teach and assess every academic standard, as the illusion of doing so would require more days and hours than are allocated to any school (Marzano & Kendall, 1998). Instead, teachers and leaders must embrace power standards (Great Schools Partnership, 2013; Ainsworth, 2003), that subset of standards that have the greatest impact on student achievement—assessments that are brief, focused, and provide immediate feedback for students and teachers.

The risk, of course, is that this emphasis on brevity fails to fully analyze student understanding of a subject, and therefore, leaders must choose wisely among the available options. On the one hand, an assessment might be so long and comprehensive that the leader delivers the results late to the teacher and the student doesn't use them. On the other hand, an assessment that is too short underestimates the student's proficiency. Both lead to error, but the second risk is far better than the first.

Create Time to Analyze and Use Feedback

The second obligation of education leaders is to create time for teachers to analyze and use feedback. Best practices involve formative assessments for students that accompany early dismissal the same day or a late start the next, so teachers can get together, score the assessments collaboratively, and plan appropriate instructional interventions and enrichments. Every school has faculty meeting and professional development meeting times built into the schedule; the central question for leaders is how to use this time. If leaders wish to focus professional learning on student achievement, then they must make a deliberate choice to give up traditional meetings, announcements, and workshops and replace those activities with a clear and explicit focus on student learning. There is no extra time in the day of a teacher or school leader. Every minute devoted to administrative announcements is a minute that cannot be devoted to the analysis of student learning; every minute wasted on death by PowerPoint is a minute that cannot be invested in a review of the most recent formative assessment data. Leaders must, in brief, not only decide what they wish to do but also what they will *not* do.

Monitor Teacher Responses

The third obligation of education leaders is to monitor teachers' responses to student achievement data. Note that this is dramatically different from the prevailing fear of teachers that they will be evaluated based on student data. "If my students do not perform well on tests, then I might get fired" represents the prevailing feeling of teachers who oppose data use in schools. Therefore, leaders must be explicit about how they explain the relationship of data and evaluation: no teacher is ever evaluated based on student test scores, but we are all evaluated based on how we respond to those scores.

Think of it this way: physicians are not evaluated based on the illnesses of patients who come to the hospital. Of course the patients are sick—that's why they came to the hospital. However, it is definitely reasonable to hold physicians at least partly accountable for what happens to the patients *after* they come to the hospital. For example, if patients are ill, but hospital-borne infections make them even sicker, then hospitals should be held accountable. Similarly, if any student arrives at school two grades behind grade level in reading, then teachers and administrators are not entirely at fault. However, if we fail to respond to that information—fail to give teachers more time for appropriate interventions—then we become responsible for that student's failures. This is the critical distinction for leaders—we are not responsible for the initial data about the student, but we do bear ultimate responsibility for our response to that data.

The most practical response to students who are behind in any subject is to give teachers more time for explicit instruction. Consider, for example, the progression of literacy instruction in your school. What happens to the time allocated to literacy instruction as students progress from the primary grades to intermediate grades to middle school and then to high school? Almost invariably, the time for literacy instruction declines with each step. Then take a look at literacy proficiency. With each transition to higher grade levels, literacy instruction typically declines and, not surprising, so does literacy proficiency. I am not attempting to make a universal generalization; however, I would suggest that readers consult the data from their own schools.

In this chapter, we explored the element of timeliness in grading and the practices teachers can use to deliver feedback in a timely way. The next chapter offers specific time-saving strategies busy teachers can use to support effective grading practices.

Chapter 9

TIME-SAVING STRATEGIES FOR BUSY TEACHERS

In this chapter, we consider how effective grading strategies save time for busy teachers. We must challenge the notion that traditional grading policies are as efficient as they appear. In fact, grading practices that lead to higher levels of student failure not only have enormous costs for the student in terms of frustration and academic distress but also cost teachers and schools excessive time and energy. By contrast, effective grading practices save time and are, therefore, in the best interests of both students and teachers. In particular, we consider the menu system, a grading practice that I have used with students ranging from elementary to graduate school. This represents one of many possible ways that teachers can save time and also provide feedback to students in a way that is fair, accurate, specific, and timely.

Finding the Time

Any new policy, whether it has to do with grading, curriculum, assessment, discipline, or any other education issue, does not have a prayer of implementation if it attempts to cram additional tasks into the days of teachers who are already overwhelmed with initiatives. In a U.S. study, University of Pennsylvania researchers Richard Ingersoll and David Perda (2009) find that, contrary to many stereotypes about teacher dissatisfaction (for example, inadequate pay, poor discipline, standardized testing), the greatest source of dissatisfaction is the lack of time to do their jobs well.

In fact, many grading reforms are stopped in their tracks because teachers assume that any policy that encourages students to do more and better work, as a consequence, requires more time and work from the teacher. Consider the case of alternative consequences for missing work. When a student fails to complete a homework assignment, the fastest thing for a teacher to do is enter zero points in the gradebook. In the stroke of a pen or the click of a mouse button, grading that particular student's assignment is completed. That's about as fast as grading gets, isn't it?

Considered in isolation, this does seem fast, but as many readers of this book know, this is a false conclusion, because for each 0 we enter in the gradebook, there are at least four time-consuming consequences that may result.

1. A student who accumulated 0s eventually learns—perhaps through a warning letter sent to parents—that he or she is in trouble and asks the teacher for help. The vast majority of teachers offer this help—often before school, during breaks, or after school. During those conferences, the "quick" 0 doesn't appear to be such a time-saving strategy.

2. The student fails, and the teacher suffers through the remainder of the academic term with an angry, unmotivated, disengaged, and perhaps disruptive student.

3. After a course failure, the teacher may see the same student again to repeat the same class the following year. Consider your own experience with students who must repeat a class. What is the relative amount of emotional energy and time required to get those students through the class compared to students who are engaged and motivated?

4. Zeroes and the failures that accompany them can lead to overly drawn-out discussions with parents and administrators.

What is the alternative to the quick 0? Two positive alternatives can save time and improve student performance. The first is to require that students complete the work. The second is to use the menu system.

Require That Students Complete the Work

Teachers can change the consequences for missing work from zero points to the requirement that students complete the work. For example, "Randall, it appears that you've made a choice today to sit at the quiet table at lunch and complete your homework." There are many variations on this theme. In elementary school, some teachers build in fifteen to twenty minutes of unstructured time in which students earn freedom of choice. Students who do not choose to complete assigned work when it is due, by default, lose that freedom and must use the unstructured time to complete their work. For secondary school students, many times during the day—homework time, academic advisories, study halls, X blocks, lunch, and structured interventions before and after school—can be used as an immediate and appropriate consequence for missing work.

Does it work for everyone? Certainly not, but it works for a surprisingly large number of students. In one comprehensive high school, this reform, as part of a comprehensive intervention and communication plan for students who were failing, resulted in more than one thousand fewer course failures in a high school of about three thousand students (Reeves, 2006b, 2008a). Because reduced failures led to significant improvements in discipline and suspensions, teachers reported saving a great deal of time that they did not have to devote to student behavioral issues.

Use the Menu System

Another time-saving strategy is the use of a menu system for students. When students set learning goals and are able to track them in a clear and meaningful way, their achievement substantially improves (Marzano, 2007). The menu system allows students to take responsibility for their learning and assume appropriate consequences for missing work. When they fail to complete an assignment or if they do badly on a test, the result is neither student excuses nor teacher sympathy. Rather, students must take the initiative to choose something else from the menu. Consider the example in figure 9.1 (page 110) from a sixth-grade social studies course.

Student Name: _____   **Period:** _____

In this class, 900 points are required to earn an A, and 800 points are required to earn a B. You must work sufficiently hard to earn one of those two grades. For each assignment, project, and assessment, you will have a scoring rubric that includes ratings of exemplary, proficient, progressing, and not meeting standards. As outlined below, you will earn credit only for work that is completed at the exemplary and proficient levels. If your work is not at least proficient, then please work harder, and ask for assistance.

Our focus this quarter is colonial America. You must choose at least one assignment within each major category—government, geography, economics, and culture. Otherwise, you may choose any combination from the menu to earn points for the grade you wish to achieve.

1. Government

1.1 Research project (300 points for exemplary, 240 points for proficient)

1.2 Book review (100 points for exemplary, 80 points for proficient)

1.3 Article review (50 points for exemplary, 40 points for proficient)

1.4 Electronic game creation (200 points for exemplary, 160 points for proficient)

1.5 Unit tests (100 points for exemplary, 80 points for proficient)

1.6 Concept map of unit test content (50 points for exemplary, 40 points for proficient)

2. Geography

2.1 Research project (300 points for exemplary, 240 points for proficient)

2.2 Book review (100 points for exemplary, 80 points for proficient)

2.3 Article review (50 points for exemplary, 40 points for proficient)

2.4 Electronic game creation (200 points for exemplary, 160 points for proficient)

2.5 Unit tests (100 points for exemplary, 80 points for proficient)

2.6 Concept map of unit test content (50 points for exemplary, 40 points for proficient)

3. Economics

3.1 Research project (300 points for exemplary, 240 points for proficient)

3.2 Book review (100 points for exemplary, 80 points for proficient)

3.3 Article review (50 points for exemplary, 40 points for proficient)

3.4 Electronic game creation (200 points for exemplary, 160 points for proficient)

3.5 Unit tests (100 points for exemplary, 80 points for proficient)

3.6 Concept map of unit test content (50 points for exemplary, 40 points for proficient)

4. Culture

4.1 Research project (300 points for exemplary, 240 points for proficient)

4.2 Book review (100 points for exemplary, 80 points for proficient)

4.3 Article review (50 points for exemplary, 40 points for proficient)

4.4 Electronic game creation (200 points for exemplary, 160 points for proficient)

4.5 Unit tests (100 points for exemplary, 80 points for proficient)

4.6 Concept map of unit test content (50 points for exemplary, 40 points for proficient)

Figure 9.1: Sample menu system for a sixth-grade social studies class.

The Menu System at Work: Matilda and Marquez

Consider how this works in practice with two students, Matilda and Marquez. Matilda struggles with tests, but electronic games fascinate her. Although she can read well, she reads slowly, and she learns better when she focuses on information in chunks rather than attempting to absorb a great deal of content at once. She also responds well to graphic representations of information. Marquez writes for the school newspaper, loves investigating topics, and writes regularly for pleasure. The prospect of research papers is, for him, an opportunity to show the teacher what he does best. Unlike many of his peers, however, he has been alienated from electronic games.

Both students worked hard during the quarter, learning a great deal about government, geography, economics, and culture during colonial times. Matilda took all four tests, and after considerable study, she scored at the proficient level on three of them, earning 240 points, but she failed to earn points on the fourth. She created two electronic games at the exemplary level, acing the scoring rubric with games that included at least twenty player moves, with each move having a historically accurate context and consequences. This earned her another 400 points for a total of 640 points for the quarter. Matilda intended to do a book review, but she was poorly organized and had difficulty putting her thoughts together in a way that would have earned the required points.

Fortunately, Matilda was able to use the content from books, articles, class discussions, and web research to create two excellent concept maps, earning another 100 points and bringing her total to 740—only 60 points away from the first B she would earn since she started school. At the same time, she was discouraged, having failed in her attempt at the book report and, despite studying, not doing well enough on unit tests to earn credit. Ms. Sorenson, the teacher and creator of the menu, could tell that something was troubling Matilda and asked her what was wrong.

"I'm so close, but I just don't have time to do a research project, and I don't think that retaking the tests will help," Matilda replied.

"Tell me about the activities this quarter in which you learned the most and that you most enjoyed," Ms. Sorenson prompted.

"Easy," Matilda replied. "The games—I've got the software down, and I loved cramming interesting facts and unusual consequences for the players. I think the other kids learned a lot, too."

"Well," Ms. Sorenson asked, "If that's what you like and that is how you learn, then why not do another game?"

"But I only need 60 points for a B," said Matilda. "Creating a game is a lot of work!"

"There are no rules here that require you to hope for the minimum possible," Ms. Sorenson responded seriously. "If you complete your next game with the detail and thought that you invested in your first two games, you'll have—let's see—940 points, and that's a solid A for the quarter."

"But it's a lot of work!" countered Matilda.

"That is correct," Ms. Sorenson said. "I can't wait to see it."

There is no ensured happy ending to this story. Perhaps, as cynics claim, Matilda will give up, knowing that she was close but finally diverted by other activities that take precedence in the life of a frustrated adolescent who doesn't get much academic direction at home. On the other hand, perhaps the engagement, excitement, and sense of controlling the learning environment created by the assignment menu allow Matilda to earn the same grade as Marquez. Thanks to lots of experience, excellent reading ability, and homework regimens his parents enforce every night, this young man will ace his tests, complete at least one research project, and have time left over to create a game, even though it's beyond what he needs for his usual grade of A. The point of the assignment menu is not to make every student do the same work but rather to engage every student in the value of the work ethic, organization, and resilience.

The menu system is not a panacea. Although it is structured so that students must learn something about each of the major curriculum areas for that quarter, the truth is that some students overinvest time in content they are interested in and underinvest time in topics that bore them. As Ms. Sorenson knows, however, that's precisely what happened when she used her previous regimen of lectures, group activities, worksheets, quizzes, and tests. Sometimes, homework compliance was below 40 percent, and if compliance meant actually using homework to learn something, then it might have been in the single digits. The menu liberated students and teachers to make choices and select learning goals. The range of activities engaged nearly every student, and the rigor of the scoring rubrics caused students to learn deeply about the topics they selected.

Challenges to the Menu System

Teachers often express two concerns about the menu system. The first is, "What if students wait until the last week to turn everything in?" That's a fair concern, and it is not unreasonable to establish deadlines throughout the term. If students miss a deadline, they can still find something else on the menu rather than turn in late work. Of course, the best situation is when students determine that it is in their own best interest to finish work properly and on time; in fact, they can earn an A before the term is over, giving them something that students crave: freedom and control over their own time.

That leads to the second teacher concern—what if students finish their work too early? That is indeed a possibility, particularly for high-performing students who know how to "play school" very well. The challenge for teachers is how to motivate these students beyond simply gaining yet another appearance on the honor roll. That is why choice, engagement, and creativity are all vital elements of the menu system. Ask teachers if they would be happier to cut the amount of grading that they have to do at the end of the semester, and I think most will be enthusiastic about the menu system.

Documenting Time-Saving Ideas

Having students complete missing work and the menu system are just two of many strategies teachers can use to save time and improve student performance. Teachers and leaders should make a regular practice of identifying, documenting, and sharing time-saving ideas. This is the starting point for any instructional initiative. A new idea, no matter how promising, is doomed to drown in a cesspool of cynicism and distrust if it begins with extra work for teachers and administrators. By contrast, if we begin each new idea by first creating time and space for it to be nurtured and grow, then we have created an environment of credibility, authenticity, and optimism, the essential nutrients of any instructional initiative.

The following chapter examines some of the risks involved in including student voices in grading practices. It also explores increased student engagement as a positive result of including students in the grading process.

Chapter 10

STUDENT VOICES IN GRADING PRACTICES

Two seemingly opposite risks are involved in including student voices in discussions of grading practices. The first is that students, seeking the easy road, might attempt to influence grading practices in a way that leads to less work, easier grades, and the maximum amount of student-selected fun rather than teacher-selected work. The second risk is that students, seeking to protect their status as high achievers, might attempt to influence grading practices in a way that leads to more work (at least for the vast majority of students), harder grades, and the maximum amount of teacher-selected work, provided that these student advocates understand what that work is and how to achieve it successfully. Neither group represents students as a whole, but the latter group is more articulate, more politically connected, and ultimately more persuasive.

I've heard few students in the top 10 percent of their class advocate for making the recognition of academic success easier. This is particularly true when academic recognition is a scarce and valuable resource linked to college scholarships. There is an active disincentive for students who receive these benefits to help anyone else enter their exclusive club. This situation presents a dilemma for teachers and school leaders who wish to grant students a voice in deliberations surrounding grading policies. The questions are, "Whose voice?" and "What do we do when students fail to advocate for themselves?"

Hypotheses About Student Engagement

If we expect students to be engaged in classroom learning, then they must be partners with teachers and not their adversaries or subordinates. When we enlist students as partners in learning and assessment practices, we have the opportunity to improve student performance and engagement. Rather than follow a prescription based on the familiar statement that "research says," we are better served if we express and test hypotheses.

Hypotheses are testable "if . . . , then . . ." statements. For example, if students find classwork engaging and relevant, then they are more likely to participate in class and complete assignments. Although this sounds obvious, it is not, as any teacher will attest. Many reasons can lead to student disengagement from classroom work, and these may having nothing to do how relevant or engaging the assignments are.

I have designed assignments for students of immigrant families that were directly relevant and engaging. Some years, these classroom activities resulted in exceptionally high engagement; but other years, the same assignments—presented to very similar students—failed to engage them. Teacher effort is part of the equation, but events in the students' lives outside the classroom—perhaps family strife, legal troubles, the risk of dislocation, relationship issues, and various other challenges—can work against the relationship I hope to establish directly with my students. That does not excuse me from trying to establish relevant and engaging classroom activities; it only explains why the best-laid plans of hard-working teachers do not always work out as planned. So it is with grading practices.

While my experience suggests that student engagement in grading practices is likely to help students understand the purpose and function of grading and its relationship to effective feedback, I could be wrong. The best way to test these hypotheses is to conduct a pilot project in which a few teachers who are willing to make student engagement in grading practices a part of their classroom routine compare their results with their colleagues.

We gather hypotheses about students and grading practices not because every hypothesis is equally valid but because every hypothesis must be tested and then, based on the best available evidence, either embraced or discarded.

Student Voices Across Grade Levels

While secondary school students may be more likely to express their wishes about grading practices, those in earlier grades, particularly primary grades, have little opportunity to do so. Indeed, their desire to please parents and teachers may be unlikely to represent their genuine desires. What we can do, however, is observe in an objective manner what students in earlier grades actually do. For example, when we express a hypothesis for how a particular activity is related to student engagement—such as tending to the needs of desert tortoises, measuring an athletic field, or synchronizing dance steps—we can fairly and objectively observe what students do in unstructured time, such as recess. I've watched students do all of these things, not because they were required to do so, but because they loved the activity. None of these actions involved extra credit or any other pursuit of a reward from the teacher or a mark in the gradebook. When given unstructured time, students make independent choices about their actions.

A quiet observation of their actions provides exceptionally helpful feedback for teachers and administrators about what students actually value. Do they spend time playing? What do they talk about? Do they spend time reading? What are their choices during unstructured time? Students certainly need unstructured time during the day, and it is tremendously informative for teachers when we take a few moments to observe student choices. How does this inform grading practices for younger students?

While I am certainly not suggesting that teachers grade students for their recess activities, it is entirely appropriate, when teachers are forming their professional judgments and assessments throughout the year, that they consider all the times that students demonstrate evidence of proficiency and mastery. For example, at Cairo American College in Egypt, I noticed students using playground time to work with a project on desert tortoises. Students carefully measured food and water, inspected each tortoise, and made notes in their field journals. When it comes time for teachers to evaluate these students' measurements, observations, writing, and math calculations, they should certainly be free to include these observations as evidence of student proficiency or extraordinary performance.

When Students, Parents, and Teachers Disagree

Clarion calls for evidence notwithstanding, two people with different perspectives and predispositions can look at the same evidence and draw different conclusions. How can we reconcile the deep-seated beliefs of some teachers, parents, and students that grading as punishment works with other equally firm convictions that grading as punishment does not work? How can educators and school leaders reconcile the evidence when, for example, one source claims that "there is no empirical evidence that policies against 0s work" (Zwaagstra, 2012) and another source provides that actual empirical evidence (Reeves, 2012a)? The response to these disagreements has two levels.

The most helpful response is for all parties involved to first agree to submit their alternative points of view to testing by mutually agreed-on tests of their hypotheses. These tests might be a review of student grades, graduation rates, performance on formative and summative assessments, or other indicators on which the parties agree. For example, when alternative consequences for missing homework are applied in controlled conditions, either the failure rate improves or it doesn't. When alternative responses to formative assessments are applied, then either performance on the summative assessment improves or it doesn't. These are not matters of speculation but of fact.

However, what happens when both sides of a controversy cannot agree on evidence or the evidentiary standard each side proposes is unpersuasive to the other? These sorts of quandaries are not without precedent. Policy often trails after science. For example, engineers used the meter as a standard length of measurement for buildings and bridges even as authorities debated the extent to which this scientific advance was consistent with their political views. Anti-miscegenation laws were nullified two centuries after Thomas Jefferson, by his own actions, found them without merit. In general, policy does not precede science but follows it, often at a distance. This explains why some of the most powerful politicians insist on teaching both sides of scientific questions, even after the evidence is settled. It is as if education policymakers in one part of the world wanted to teach both sides of the gravity question, because they feared that opposition from groups against the theory of gravity would feel disrespected.

Many argue that education is as much art as science. But the acknowledgment of the uncertain boundaries of art does not diminish the clear advances in science. Each generation of students, teachers, and policymakers depends on the rest of us to recognize the difference.

If we expect students to engage meaningfully in discussions about grading practices, then we must include them in the process. The tradition of distributing a syllabus and grading policy should give way to an open and honest discussion of alternative grading practices. While students do not necessarily vote on the outcome—effective grading practices are not always popular—we can listen to what they have to say and offer them a better understanding of the policies that influence their grades. The next chapter examines what education leaders can do to support and lead the change in grading policies.

Chapter 11

LEADING CHANGE FOR EFFECTIVE GRADING POLICIES

"But who is going to tie the bell on the cat?" So ends the tale of the council of wise mice who were unanimous in their opinion that the threatening cat should have a bell tied around its neck, a solution that all agreed would make sense, save the lives of mice, and not harm the cat. Unfortunately, however thoughtful and rational their deliberations, the mice were unable to move from policy to implementation. Such moves require courage and the willingness to confront risks. So it is with grading policies. Being right is not enough. Having the preponderance of evidence on your side is insufficient. In fact, establishing mathematical certainty is of scant comfort when emotion, righteous indignation, and indifference to evidence are stacked against you.

The most common question I receive from audiences around the world begins with the phrase, "How do I convince . . . ?" The disappointing answer is that you don't. You do not persuade merely with research, evidence, and logic. The evidence for improved grading policies has been around for almost a century. Rather than mere logic and facts, we need a thoughtful process for implementing policy changes, and that is what this chapter offers.

Leaders must create a mission for schools and education systems. While these missions typically include commitments to universal student learning and engagement, as well as the inclusion of 21st century skills, it is often difficult to reconcile these mission statements with a school's day-to-day policies. This is particularly true with the differences between mission statements and grading policies. For example, if we aspire to encourage student creativity and collaboration, but our grading policies fail to include these skills, then the stated mission is meaningless. If we aspire to teach students a good work ethic, but punish them if they fail to get work done right the first time, then we are teaching students that responding to feedback and working harder as a result is futile. This chapter suggests how leaders can close the gap between rhetoric and reality.

Defining the Purposes of Grading

One of the most perplexing elements of debates over grading policies is how very intelligent and rational people can look at the same set of facts and come to radically different conclusions. Perhaps the root cause for this phenomenon is that there are widely differing perspectives on the fundamental purposes of grading. These generally fall into the following categories.

- Giving feedback to students in order to improve their performance
- Reporting to parents on student progress toward specific learning objectives
- Communicating with teachers at the next level of instruction so they can plan instruction in a way that meets a variety of student learning needs
- Rewarding students for good behavior and attitudes
- Punishing students for poor behavior and attitudes
- Making public distinctions between good students and bad students

While most educators would agree that the first three purposes (feedback, reporting, and communication) are the most important purposes of grading, it does not take very long for most discussions of grading policies to reveal that the last three (rewards, punishments, and distinction) are at the heart of most grading policies. The telltale phrases that reflect this conclusion include the following, paraphrased from many conversations and email exchanges I have had with teachers and school administrators on the subject of grading.

- I know that she didn't meet the academic standard, but how else am I supposed to recognize that she tried hard, came to class, and finished her homework? Honor roll grades are the only recognition that poor kid will ever get!

- He's not even sorry for missing his assignments! His attitude is casual and contemptuous. I don't care if he aced the end-of-course exam—he's failing my class until he shows some contrition. (Contrition is a theme that features prominently with my correspondents who find punitive grading as the last tool available to teachers.)

- If I let some students submit their work after correcting it, it's not fair to the other students who got it right the first time.

Giving Rewards and Punishments

Pink (2009) and Kohn (1999) build strong cases that rewards and punishments, like those used to induce rats to find their way through a maze, are not effective ways to encourage learning. In fact, there is substantial evidence that other variables, including respect, mastery, autonomy, and pursuit of worthy goals, are far more motivating than rewards and punishments. Even when rewards and punishments do influence human behavior, they sometimes have unintended consequences. For example, rewarding teachers for high test scores does not necessarily encourage improved student results but rather provides a direct incentive for experienced teachers to migrate from economically disadvantaged schools to wealthy ones (Haycock & Crawford, 2008).

Rewarding teachers for growth in test scores—an attempt to induce teachers to stay in poor schools—can unintentionally provide an incentive to focus only on the least mobile students who are right below the level of proficiency. Highly mobile students, or those far below and far above proficiency, need effective teaching too, but if we accept the behavioral theory of rewards and punishments, then those students are sacrificed to the prevailing incentive system. These rewards, in other words, miss their targets and fail to achieve their intended results.

The same is true when grades are used as rewards and punishments. Guskey (2015) provides impressive evidence that can be summarized in a single sentence—grading as punishment does not work. In fact, when students are rewarded only with feedback on their performance and are not subjected to a grade, their performance is better than when they are graded. Similarly, when teachers think that they are building work ethic and respect by using 0s for missing work, strict policies against accepting resubmitted work, and the average to determine final grades, rather than encouraging work ethic and personal responsibility, they send a clear message—your semester is over after a few missing assignments, so you might as well give up.

One of the most common beliefs related to student grading policies are that students respond to threats and punishment. That is the essence of the claims of teachers who, as Zwaagstra (2012) reports, believe that draconian penalties lead to improved performance, making students think carefully about turning in work that is late or inadequate or, worst of all, failing to complete work. While even a cursory review of the research on student motivation reveals that grading as punishment does not work (Guskey, 2015) and alternative consequences for missing work are dramatically effective (Reeves, 2012b), the predominant hypothesis from students is that they are rats in Skinner's box, responding to punishments and rewards on cue. This is why we should, in a democratic society, welcome the views of students, parents, and the public, but also why we should distinguish between claims and evidence.

But evidence alone is insufficient, particularly when it is associated with students and education systems unfamiliar to the teachers who are considering changes in grading policies. That is why hypotheses are not tested in the library but in the real world of classrooms, schools, and systems. Ideally, two competing and mutually exclusive hypotheses should be considered. The first hypothesis might suggest that if students fail to complete homework and are penalized with Fs and 0s, then the threat of these sanctions improve their performance, homework completion, final grades, and academic proficiency.

The alternative hypothesis might suggest that if students fail to complete homework and are required to complete the work in alternative settings, such as the quiet table at lunch or the coach's corner (a Friday morning group for students who have not finished homework), then the threat of these sanctions improves their performance, homework completion, final grades, and academic proficiency. Both of these alternative hypotheses can be tested in the same school with the same classes, same curriculum, same (or very similar) teachers, same final exams, and same measures of academic proficiency. The only differences are the consequences for missing, late, and inadequate student work.

These sorts of carefully conducted observations are far superior to heartfelt beliefs of distant academics. It is not the intensity of the beliefs of those who express hypotheses that matters; it is the evidence based on repeated trials. Ultimately, repetition of these observations yields a widely spread consensus in the professional community. For example, there was a time in the not too distant past when corporal punishment "improved" student behavior. The preponderance of the evidence on corporal punishment has not dissuaded some teachers, administrators, parents, and policymakers from their convictions that this form of improvement is a good idea, but almost any fair reading of the evidence would conclude the opposite.

When much of the grade depends on homework, home projects, and other factors that presume effective parental supervision and a stable home environment, there is another clear message that students receive—you better be very careful in selecting your parents. If you go home to an attentive and academically encouraging home environment, you will be rewarded. If, on the other hand, you go home to the chaos of unemployment, preoccupation, relocation, or a hundred other social and family dysfunctions, then the impact of those factors on your academic performance and homework completion will be regarded as a sign of laziness, inattentiveness, and inability to complete academic work.

I don't think the vast majority of teachers would agree that these ideas reflect their intentions. If that is the case, then let us proceed to a discussion of grading policies that has as its first principle: the primary purpose of grading is feedback to students to improve performance. We also should agree in explicit terms, as a matter of policy, that rewards and punishments for attitudes and behavior, along with the creation of distinctions among students, are not acceptable purposes for grading. Most educators and administrators agree that, when it comes to educational accountability for schools, the primary purpose is to improve teaching and learning. They would further agree that it is ineffective and counterproductive to use test scores and accountability policies to rate, sort, humiliate, and publicly rank teachers, administrators, and schools. These same strong beliefs must, therefore, be applied to grading policies.

Implementing Unpopular Policy Changes

Education leaders must make difficult policy decisions all the time, and in a democracy, one of the criteria for these decisions is the will of a majority of voters. This leads many leaders to make buy-in the principal factor that they weigh in establishing education policy. However, let us take care before we accept this premise. For example, consider a school board who approved, by a three-to-one margin, the installation of a sprinkler system in the elementary school, a decision that brought the school into compliance with state fire code requirements. What if the vote had gone the other way? Are we willing to stipulate that the will of the majority is a value superior to students' safety?

Progress in education, from ending segregation to the implementation of evidence-based leadership and teaching practices, has not always been the result of buy-in from staff members or the will of the electorate majority. Rather, effective educational change is often the result of visionary leadership that, against all odds and significant resistance, elevates essential values over popularity.

Education is not the only field in which innovation, progress, and change happen without popular support. In fields as diverse as brain surgery and social work, agriculture and investment banking, prison reform and emergency room medicine, and water purification and the piloting of passenger aircraft, buy-in has little impact on consistently creating organizational change (Kotter, 1996, 2008). The most obvious public policies—such as not allowing train, plane, and automobile operators to use computers and smartphones while operating life-threatening equipment—are debated, opposed, and delayed. Evidence is not enough, and buy-in is an illusion.

Rather, an emerging consensus in change leadership literature (Fullan, 2011; Deutschman, 2007; Fullan, 2008a; Gawande, 2009; Heath & Heath, 2010; Patterson et al., 2008) suggests a new model for practical change. The missing elements, these authors propose, include specific behavioral change at the individual level.

Chip and Dan Heath (2010) suggest, for example, that goals that are too general leave too much for individual interpretation. *Be healthy*, to use one example, is not as effective as *drink skim milk*. Patterson and colleagues (2008) illustrate the same need for specificity in the context of world health, showing how generic programs spend hundreds of millions of dollars, but small, behavior-oriented programs focused on clear and specific objectives achieve what mammoth programs cannot in preventing disease in developing nations. Gawande's (2009) clarion call for checklists makes clear that even in the most sophisticated professional, corporate, educational, and governmental enterprises, clarity of expectations is at the heart of the new wave of change efforts.

Four-Level, Action-Oriented Change Model

I will now introduce a four-level, action-oriented change model that can be used to implement changes in grading policies. The same procedure also can be used widely in education. The elements of the model include: (1) explicit vision, (2) specification of behavior, (3) assessment and feedback, and (4) continuous refinement.

Explicit Vision

The leader must first create an explicit vision. This is not the gauzy illusion often associated with corporate vision statements but an architect's vision that mobilizes many different people toward a common aim. The vision is clear, specific, and as vivid as the most vibrant painting or sculpture. Do not begin your consideration of grading policies with a generalized discussion. That procedure leads only to hardened positions and commitments to present practice. Rather, begin the discussion with consideration of student failures and successes. Create two alternative visions, one in which you continue with present trends and a second in which fewer students fail and more students succeed. Invite your colleagues to brainstorm answers to the following questions.

- How would our school be different if we had fewer student failures?

- What would it mean to us if we had fewer students in our classes who were repeating the class for the second or third time?

- If we did not have so many resources diverted to course repetition, what new electives could we offer?

- What course or topic have we always wanted to teach but never had time to teach?

- If we had fewer failures, fewer suspensions, fewer expulsions, and even fewer low-level discipline problems, how would our professional and personal lives be better?

We must have a vivid, explicit, and compelling vision in order to ignite difficult changes, whether the challenge at hand is reducing infant mortality, reducing criminal recidivism, or improving student success. Change is too difficult, and reversion to prevailing behavior is too easy, without a compelling vision.

Specification of Behavior

The leader must then create explicit behavioral expectations for implementing the change. Note that the leader does not say, "I would like you to *believe* in this way," as it is too early in the process to change belief systems. All the leader says is, "I would like you to do the following things in the following very specific ways. I know that everyone may not agree yet that this is the right course of action, but

I want us to try it out, assess our results, and then see if we agree that it was a risk worth taking."

In the context of grading policy, then, the discussion might sound like this: "We agreed that it is essential for us to reduce course failures, and if we are successful, we will achieve a vision that includes more student success, improved discipline, and a significantly better professional environment for the faculty. In order to achieve that vision, we are making two clear and immediate changes. First, the consequences for missing assignments or turning in low-quality work will no longer be zero points or grades of F but rather a requirement that students complete the work. We will collaborate to create time, support, and appropriate consequences, including time before, during, and after school for students to finish their work. To be clear, we will no longer use the 0 on a one hundred–point scale. We will no longer use the average to calculate the final grade. Our objective is not to give grades away but to create an environment in which students earn higher grades and have fewer failures because they worked harder, respected teacher feedback, and completed their work at a higher level of quality than in the past."

Assessment and Feedback

Next, the leader must assess the implementation of instructional initiatives and identify the level of implementation of these practices and its impact on improved student results. It is simply not true that people either implement a policy or fail to implement it. There is, in almost every complex educational matter, a range of successful implementations. When it comes to grading policies, the range might look something like the following.

- **Level 1:** The teacher receives the research and professional development on grading policies but does not implement new practices in the classroom. There remains evidence of 0s, averages, and the use of grades to reward and punish student attitudes and behaviors. There is no evidence that low-performing students are using the feedback from grades to improve their performance. Leaders fail to participate in or observe the results of this professional learning.

- **Level 2:** Teachers have somewhat revised classroom grading policies, with late work and revisions to low-quality work accepted, but the prevailing expectation is that work is done only at home. There is little evidence of students using feedback for improved performance. Leaders are complacent, accepting present practices.

- **Level 3:** Classroom grading policies meet the school standards, and there is clear evidence of opportunity before, during, and after school for students to improve and complete work. The teacher reports a significant improvement in the quantity and quality of student work, and there is a measurable and significant decline in student failure. Moreover, the improvement in student academic performance is leading to an improved classroom environment. Leaders are active participants in the process, coaching teachers, praising their efforts, and acknowledging with enthusiasm the improved student performance.

- **Level 4:** All of level 3 criteria are met, and the teacher also has developed innovative structures to assist underperforming students and challenge high-achieving students. Moreover, the teacher has implemented innovative structures to encourage higher levels of student performance, improved personal organization, and the timely (or even early) submission of required student work. The teacher is also experimenting with "risk-free" assignments in which the sole goal is learning, not achieving a grade, and is sharing the promising results of this action research project with colleagues. Leaders empower teachers to share their best practices with colleagues throughout the system and implement large-scale systemic change.

This is, of course, only a first draft. Early in any change process, it will be apparent that the change works for some people and not for others. Specifications that are crystal clear to the leader are murky to some faculty members. That is why the next level of this change model is necessary.

Continuous Refinement

After assessing the degree of implementation of the change and the impact of those changes on student results, the leader must refine and improve results on a continuous basis. The reason for implementation variations almost always has to do with differences in how various staff members take the same policy, same training, same technology tools, and same leadership guidance and apply them in different ways. While sometimes active resistance accounts for these differences in implementation, a far more common cause is the failure of leadership to specify with sufficient clarity exactly what change behaviors are expected.

In the context of grading, this discussion might sound like the following. "Mr. Walters, in my last visit to the class, I noticed that four students failed to complete the assignment for the day, but it was not clear to me how you would handle that situation. Could you please explain how the work will be completed and what support from me, if any, you may need to ensure that these students get back on track?"

Another conversation might go as follows: "Ms. Smith, I noticed that to calculate the progress report for your students, you were using the computer default of the average of scores to calculate students' grades. I know that the computer does this automatically, but I really trust your judgment about how students are performing right now. This is what I would like to see you do not only now but for the final grades. Can I count on you to do this?"

These conversations may strike some readers as focusing on an excessive level of detail, but it is indeed this level of detail that is absent in many grading-policy improvements as well as in most areas of change leadership. Leaders undermine their own best intentions time and again when they equivocate. One common temporization goes like this: "The leader is just articulating the vision, but of course, each school and classroom teacher must determine how best to achieve that vision." This is a prescription for failure, as it suggests that implementation is divorced from achieving goals. What teachers do, from classroom feedback to lesson planning to curriculum articulation to grading policies, is not a matter of personal taste but of effective implementation that requires clarity and specificity. Many areas of teacher discretion remain, such as engaging scenarios for lessons and assessments, but grading policies or any other education reform will not achieve improved results if implementation specification is left to chance.

Aligning Systemic Support

Most change initiatives result not in systemic change but in *islands of excellence* (Reeves, 2008b), in which change is demonstrably effective at the individual classroom or school level, while districtwide change remains elusive. Fullan (2010) makes a compelling case for systems alignment. Because schools and school systems are organizationally complex, change in one part of the system—such as improved grading policies—can have a significant impact on all other parts of the system, improving failure rates, discipline, morale, equity, college opportunities, and more. On the other hand, failure to have adequate system alignment undermines even the most straightforward policy.

Examine Evaluation Systems

Consider the example of teacher and administrator evaluation. Most systems have explicit and implicit evaluation systems. The explicit evaluation systems have little impact on performance (DuFour & Marzano, 2009). Moreover, the evaluation process for both teachers and administrators is a lethargic one, in which feedback occurs long after the instructional and leadership behaviors those evaluations were to influence occurred.

Not only does the explicit evaluation system fail to support change or sanction the failure to change, the implicit evaluation system can actively contradict change messages. Whereas formal policies and negotiated forms govern explicit evaluation systems, implicit evaluation systems—the daily conversations among administrators, peers, parents, and other sources of influence—have no such defined boundaries. Any careful observer, however, can identify the prevailing trends in implicit evaluation systems. One of the most common trends is the systemic preference for tranquility and an absence of conflict and complaint. Therefore, the vociferous complaints of a handful of faculty, parents, administrators, or community members can sometimes be interpreted as "a lot of people are complaining." Because the implicit message is that complaints are bad and the absence of complaints is good, it is important to establish one essential fact at the outset of any grading policy change: complaints are inevitable, even when your change is successful and student achievement is improving.

When there are fewer failures, many good things happen, including improvements in discipline, achievement, and opportunity. However, improved opportunities for more students to take honor and advanced classes mean, at least in the short term, that those classes have higher enrollments than they did in the past, and that the composition of those classes is more diverse. Parents (and perhaps a few teachers) who were used to relatively small advanced classes, occupied by students who have traditionally been among the academic elite, may find these changes disconcerting.

This becomes a particular problem for leaders when influential and well-connected parents carry their complaints to senior administrative and board of education levels. An elected official's immediate priority is to solve a constituent's problem. The senior administrator's impulsive reaction is to avoid a controversy with a board member, but those reactions, however reasonable and common, are precisely what create tension between the system's values and goals and the implicit evaluation system and all that it entails.

What can leaders do to achieve better alignment with their implicit evaluation systems? First, they must identify exactly what those implicit messages are and determine whether or not they are congruent with the essential goals of leadership. While elected officials, including members of boards of education, must be sensitive to complaints from constituents, policymaking inevitably involves trade-offs. Pursuing one goal diminishes the achievement of another, particularly if one of those goals is heavily invested in preserving current policies. It is not that leaders and elected officials cannot cope with complaints; my experience suggests, instead, that they prefer to anticipate rather than react to these complaints.

When system leaders change policies, they must be alert to potential complaints and let senior administrators and policymakers know what to expect. The response of, "Thanks for your concern. We have actually anticipated that, and here is why we think it's a good idea . . ." is much more protective of stakeholder relationships than a surprised, "Thanks for your concern. I'll have to look into that and get back to you." The latter suggests that there is a problem to be solved; the former suggests that, while the concern may be legitimate, it does not outweigh the other policy priorities that leaders have already considered.

Resolve Disagreements

Of course, not all policy matters are resolved when both sides see the merit of their opposition, withdraw their objections, and live happily ever after. A pluralistic society guarantees diverse points of view. That is its strength, and realistic system leaders acknowledge that the resolution of disagreements is not always a matter of negotiation, mutual concessions, and ultimate agreement. Sometimes, we simply agree to disagree and move on in the best interest of the organization.

One of the most important interview questions to ask aspiring administrators, superintendents, and teachers is, "What has happened in the past when you had a disagreement with your colleagues? What were the issues? How did you resolve them? If the issues were not resolved, what did you do?" Although I have asked many candidates this question, most people are surprised at the inquiry, and even otherwise outstanding candidates dissemble a bit.

The fact is that, particularly in education, we have not done a particularly good job of articulating how we resolve disagreements. The authoritarian "my way or the highway" response is a splendid management philosophy when the building is on fire. Command and control are essential when immediate compliance is required. However, few other issues in the daily lives of teachers and administrators rise to the level of "The building is on fire, and I need you to do what I'm asking you to do, no questions asked, right now." These are what we might call *safety* and *value* issues, which get to the heart of the first mission of school systems: safeguarding the lives—physical, emotional, and intellectual—of the students entrusted to us.

When we see adults threaten the lives and well-being of students, whether by throwing a lit cigarette into a wastebasket, striking a child, or engaging in practices that seem destructive, then we have an obligation to stop it. Unfortunately, leaders too rarely distinguish the vital issues worthy of this sort of emotional investment and personal confrontation from other issues. Moreover, because leaders often concentrate their conversations and intellectual energy on their own requirements, they fail to invest similar energy in those areas where they do *not* have mandates and where teachers can exercise professional discretion.

One effective way of resolving disagreements before they get out of control is creating a clear decision-making framework, one that includes those decisions that are up to the classroom teacher's discretion (type 1), those that are subject to collaboration among teachers and administrators (type 2), and those that senior leadership has made or will make and classroom teachers and building administrators must execute (type 3). In a series of surveys (Reeves, 2006a), I first asked respondents from a variety of schools in Canada and the United States to estimate the percentage of decisions that fell into each type. Not surprisingly, most respondents thought very few decisions (4 percent) fell into the first type, teacher discretion. The respondents speculated that a few more decisions were collaborative (22 percent). They predicted that a vast majority of education decisions (74 percent) were the result of administrative dictates.

Then, to get a reality check on these assumptions, I gave the same respondents equal amounts of time to record all of the classroom and school decisions that they could think of for each category. The results were surprising, with 39 percent of the actual decisions falling into teacher discretion. Fewer of the decisions (34 percent) were collaborative, leaving only 27 percent for those that were made in a hierarchical, top-down, command-and-control manner.

These results were so surprising that many people, including those whose own data contributed to the findings, could barely believe the results. "Everything we do is micromanaged," they countered. "These results can't be right!" Perhaps you have the same reaction, so rather than argue over whether or not that particular survey applies to you, consider conducting an experiment.

Identify some act of teaching or instructional leadership that, at least on the surface, appears to be uniform. Perhaps at 9:30 a.m., there should be guided reading in every second-grade classroom. Perhaps during every PLC meeting, there should be an explicit examination of individual and classroom-level data and a consideration of alternative teaching strategies to improve student results. Keep it simple, with an expectation that is so clear, so explicit, and so consistent that you have a high degree of confidence in finding uniform results. Then, make some systematic observations. At 9:30 a.m., go to five different second-grade classrooms, and see if your observations reveal the uniformity of practice you expected. Visit five collaborative team meetings, and simply count the frequency of those that met your expectation of data analysis and evaluation of teaching strategies.

One of the most persistent and important findings a range of researchers report—including John Hattie (2012), John Hattie and Gregory Yates (2014), Gerald Bracey (2005), Mike Schmoker (2005, 2006), William Sanders (1998), Linda Darling-Hammond and Gary Sykes (1999), and many others—is that the most significant variation is not from one school system to another, or even one school to another, but from one classroom to another.

Kim Marshall (2009), in the important book *Rethinking Teacher Supervision and Evaluation*, offers specific tools for observing similarities and differences in teaching practices. The application of Marshall's tools reveals, in many cases, striking differences in daily classroom practices. Sometimes those differences may be due to varied levels of professional knowledge, but in the vast majority of cases, differences in teaching and leadership are reflections of personal decisions. "That's just the way I do things," teachers and administrators explain.

Therefore, resolving differences is not a matter of rhetoric, evidence, professional learning, or stern administrative warnings. Rather, leaders must identify which differences of opinion and practice are worthy of the emotional and leadership energy required to resolve them. The three-level, decision-making typology is a good way to start. First, identify the type 1 decisions in which teachers have discretion. Second, identify the type 2 decisions in which the final result is collaboration between teachers and administrators. Third, identify the type 3 decisions that genuinely represent factors that influence the students' safety and the values of the education system.

A great deal of what happens in the classroom is a type 1 decision, a matter of the teacher's minute-to-minute discretion. Type 2 decisions include those that depend on the collaborative efforts of teachers, such as the common formative assessments that they periodically provide for all students. Type 3 decisions should be limited to matters of the highest importance, those issues in which leaders must exercise their authority to ensure student welfare. For example, safety issues, such as crossing guards, cafeteria hygiene, and playground equipment, are not matters of individual taste but of system-level policy. We can make the case that reducing student failure by removing ineffective grading policies is also a safety issue, because students who fail academically and ultimately drop out of school suffer risks that adversely influence their health and the economic viability of the United States (Alliance for Excellent Education, 2010).

It can be useful for leaders to show stakeholders that their district is certainly not the only education system to engage in grading reform. In the appendix (page 163), you will find a sample grading policy from the American International School Riyadh (2014–2015) that is certainly not perfect but is very thoughtful and proceeds from purpose to policy.

You also may access a number of different grading policies as well as report cards from other districts across the United States. Visit **go.solution-tree.com/assessment** to access the links to these materials. The report cards are not perfect, but they represent a genuine improvement in the way schools report student progress to parents and students. Leaders must ultimately craft report cards that represent their vision about the value of feedback and the necessity that grading policies and report cards are FAST—fair, accurate, specific, and timely.

So far, I have addressed the grading policies for a significant majority of students—those involved in regular education classes. However, what about the significant number of students with special needs? In the next chapter, I will emphasize that students with special needs require the same elements of grading as their regular education peers. That is, their grading policies must be fair, accurate, specific, and timely.

Chapter 12

GRADING FOR STUDENTS WITH SPECIAL NEEDS

In a growing number of nations, there are specific protections for the rights of students with special needs. In general, schools provide for adaptations and accommodations for these students. When a student in a wheelchair cannot reach the lab surface in the science room or the dictionary stand in the library, the accommodations required are straightforward. In physical education classes, the same wheelchair-bound student can engage actively in strategy, competition, cardiovascular exercise, and virtually every class activity. Indeed, as the Paralympics have demonstrated, there is no contradiction in the term *wheelchair athlete*. However, the issue of adaptation and accommodation becomes considerably more complex when schools attempt to use traditional grading practices for students with a wide range of physical, neurological, and emotional challenges.

The best guidance for schools on the application of grading to students with special needs is based on the principles with which we began this book: grades must be fair, accurate, specific, and timely.

Fairness

In the context of students with special needs, fairness and accuracy are inextricably linked. The demand for accuracy in assessing writing, for example, implies that we focus our assessment on the quality of student writing, not the speed of writing. Our assessment of the quality of mathematical prowess is not the same as an assessment of the speed of mathematical calculation. This distinction is the reason that one of the most important adaptations for students with special needs is the availability of more time to complete the task at hand. Rather than lower teacher expectations so that a poor job is done in haste, the adaptation of time conveys the essential expectation that students can perform at high levels. The consequence for their failure to do so is neither sympathy from the teacher nor a compensatory grade ("She's in special education, so I had to give her a B") but rather the most appropriate adaptation of all—time.

In my own teaching career, I have worked with students who proceeded from fragmentary sentences to sequential lists to complete sentences to paragraphs to essays. Sometimes this process required three months; sometimes it took three years. I am not naïve about the profound difficulty that students with learning disabilities face, but neither am I dismayed nor intimidated by the fact that it takes some students longer to process information and produce results than other students.

Accuracy

In some nations, such as the United States, there is a specific requirement in federal legislation that students with special needs receive an individualized education plan (IEP) that specifies their lesson modifications, adaptations, and instructional strategies. Therefore, the most accurate way to grade students using an IEP is to use the IEP itself as the frame of reference for the report card.

If, for example, Michelle's IEP specifies eight reading objectives, an accurate report card might include the information that she fully achieved four of those objectives, partially achieved two, and did not achieve two. The report card would then explain the steps that Michelle's instructional team is collaboratively taking to create appropriate instruction modifications and further appropriate adaptations so she will continue this pursuit of standards. Note that even though Michelle did not achieve every objective, the process was not unsuccessful. The process was accurate and, therefore, allowed both the student and her teachers to make midcourse corrections to improve her education.

Think of how much more helpful this process is than the common statement, "Because Michelle had an IEP, I gave her a B in English," even though the student, teacher, and parents all know that Michelle's grade of B was based on work that was not close to other students' work that received the same grade. When the law requires that students receive an individualized curriculum and assessment, the use of letter or numerical grades—perhaps the ultimate in standardized and nonindividualized assessment—seems unwise.

Specificity

Special education teachers are masters of *incrementalization*, the process of taking a task that might have seemed to many classroom teachers as a single unit of work and breaking it down into its essential components. This is, in fact, not merely a special education technique but the essence of what outstanding coaches, teachers, executives, and performance analysts do at every level in every field. However, special education teachers bring a consistency and discipline to the process of incrementalization that is particularly useful in a discussion of effective grading practices. Rather than evaluating a single skill, such as reading comprehension, a special educator might consider enumerating the steps that Michelle has learned in order to improve her reading comprehension. These might include the following four steps.

1. **Prereading:** Finding topic sentences and gaining an initial understanding of the author's purpose

2. **Highlighting unfamiliar words:** Reducing frustration in reading passages by identifying, in advance, which words may require definitions or an attempt to understand them in context

3. **Building an idea organizer:** Visually demonstrating the relationships between facts and conclusions, causes and effects, or claims and counterclaims

4. **Summarizing:** Restating the text in her own words and checking for understanding

In fact, Michelle can read and understand challenging grade-level material, but sometimes she won't finish reading that material if she does not follow this very disciplined process approach to the text. It is not helpful for Michelle or her parents if a report card says, "Reading: C–." She may simply conclude, "See, I knew I was a bad reader." However, if the feedback on her report card is specific, Michelle then has a path to better achievement. For example, "Michelle is superior when it comes to prereading and highlighting unfamiliar words. Now, she needs to practice building idea organizers from texts. In particular, she needs to work on the following skill: identifying causes and effects." It is worth noting that, from my experience coaching many doctoral students, these same techniques that are used for effective interventions to help struggling readers can also be of immense value for graduate students struggling with complex text in their disciplines (Azar, n.d.).

Timeliness

Although feedback can have a powerful impact on student learning, the power of feedback is directly related to the timeliness with which it is provided. Because of the legal burdens associated with the documentation of meetings for special education teams, we should acknowledge that while these teams can set long-term strategies for students, they are not the right venue for providing timely feedback to improve student performance. That remains the province of the classroom and special education teachers. Therefore, it is particularly important that the daily feedback provided to students is exceptionally clear in purpose and evaluated in terms of its results.

If, for example, a student who is unable to concentrate for extended periods of time is confronted with thirty prealgebra problems as a fifth-grade homework assignment, one common adaptation might be to reduce the number of problems. This is a perfectly logical solution if and only if the reduced number of problems allows the student to nevertheless gain sufficient practice to understand the grade-level material. Of course, if a student with an IEP can gain sufficient practice with fifteen rather than thirty problems, then so can the rest of the class. It is possible, however, that the mere quantity of problems is not really addressing the problem.

For Max, another student in Michelle's class, the following problem might as well be in Sanskrit: "Find the y-intercept, where $y = mx + b$ and the slope is 2.5 . . ." Max never got past the word *intercept*. Just as with Michelle's series of paragraphs, this problem is a multipiece puzzle that must be broken down into its component parts. Perhaps Max's teacher will work on a series of steps for each problem, having students find the question and list the variables they know, the variables they don't know, and so on. In other words, having fifteen impenetrable problems rather than thirty is not the solution to the challenge Max is facing. Receiving a report card that says, "Math: B+ with adaptations" is equally unhelpful.

Max really does need to understand this problem, as it is the basis for many other tasks he will face in geometry, algebra, and statistics in future years. His success in pursuing this objective, however, requires much more from him and his teachers than simply turning in a series of shortened assignments. The grading system for Max serves him best if teachers do not attempt to use an ill-fitting standard report card with letters and numbers.

The challenge for Max and for every student is to understand with clarity and specificity what he can do, what he needs to work on, and what are the best strategies for his next steps in learning. These are the steps to success.

Students with special needs are entitled to accurate information about their academic proficiency. They deserve the same consideration we offer to any student—grading policies that are fair, accurate, specific, and timely. These need not be the same policies used in regular education, but they must not be ambiguous and leave students and parents wondering how to make progress to the next level of learning. As with all students, those with special needs should be heard and their engagement is of paramount importance. Above all, they should view grades as a form of feedback for improving learning.

The next chapter examines the impact of technology on grading practices. In many cases, technology enhances our lives. We can be, at least on the surface, more productive. However, using technology in the grading process can introduce mistakes, often on a grand scale. It is now time to make technology our servant rather than allowing it to be our master.

Chapter 13

THE IMPACT OF TECHNOLOGY ON GRADING PRACTICES

Technology is a pervasive part of almost every school environment. From one-to-one laptop initiatives to electronic displays, such as SMART Boards, to electronic adaptive testing to web-based grade-books, the impact of technology on 21st century schools can hardly be overstated. At its best, technology-assisted grading practices enhance the immediacy of feedback for students and parents. If they check the class website, students and parents know precisely where they stand, including what homework is due, what major projects are underway, when tests are scheduled, and the teacher's expectations.

Effective use of technology also allows teachers to assess their own performance, identifying which lessons and units of study were most and least successful with respect to improvements in student performance. As Hattie (2012) emphasizes, technology can be used to implement pre- and posttests to measure the impact of teaching on student learning.

On the other hand, Fullan (2013) describes how the most common use of technology is for information retrieval and the least common uses are for collaboration and modeling. Nevertheless, education systems have multibillion-dollar investments in technology, and that leads to a commitment to make more extensive use of technology throughout the system. This chapter discusses how to make wise use of promising, yet potentially ineffective, technology.

Electronic Gradebooks

Handwritten gradebooks are tedious, requiring a burst of energy by teachers several times a year, often with the application of complex and idiosyncratic formulas for determining final grades. This seems to offer an ideal platform for the systematic application of technology to a dreary manual task. Up to a point, this is correct—electronic gradebooks can save teachers time, engage parents, and offer students daily feedback on their recent and cumulative performance. However, the same electronic gradebooks can institutionalize some of the worst practices in grading, demotivating students and alienating parents.

Contemporary examples of electronic gradebook systems include Alma, Edsby, PraxiSchool, and GradeBookWizard. Almost every electronic gradebook has three common features. First, teachers enter assignments and student grades, almost always between zero and one hundred points. It might be a daily quiz with ten items or an exam, but a score between zero and one hundred points remains the prevalent way of scoring these assessments. Second, the teacher is allowed to weight each assignment, so a quiz or homework assignment might have a smaller weight, at least individually, than a final examination. Third, the electronic system calculates the final grade based on the average of student performance during the semester.

At first, this makes sense, and it even allows individual teachers some judgment with regard to the weighting of different assignments and the quantity of work to include. It's possible, for example, to include classroom participation marks in real time, while student discussions are taking place, and mark that homework is complete, all on a daily basis. This provides various stakeholders, including parents and athletic coaches, with information on how students are performing and the degree to which students are eligible for extracurricular activities. It also replaces the drill of accumulating lots of scores at the end of the grading term with steadily accumulating grades throughout the term. Ideally, students can ask at any time, "How am I doing in this class?" and they can get immediate and specific responses to that question.

If only it were that easy. For the work described in the previous paragraph, schools don't need teachers but data-entry clerks. Teachers with whom I have spoken bemoan the enormous amount of time spent in data entry that could have been devoted to providing meaningful feedback to students. The question, "How am I doing?" is far more superficial than the question, "What do I need to do in order to get to the next level?" The answer to that question from the electronic gradebook is to acquire more points, while the answer to the same question from a teaching professional is far more nuanced.

There certainly are advantages to using electronic gradebooks. This is especially true with regard to communicating with parents and students in a timely manner, so students aren't waiting until a report card is delivered to know how they are doing. In addition, electronic gradebooks help teachers and school administrators to identify which students are in danger of failure so they can provide effective interventions.

But for all the benefits of electronic gradebooks, significant liabilities still exist. If leaders and teachers do not properly control them, using this technology can perpetuate some of the worst practices in grading—0 on a one hundred–point scale and the average. This book previously made the case that 0 on a one hundred–point scale is mathematically inaccurate, magnifying the impact of missing and inadequate work and making it almost impossible for students to dig out of a hole of 0s from earlier in the semester. This sense of despair and hopelessness is compounded by the use of the average, punishing students at the end of the semester for their earlier failures. The average, in particular, punishes risk taking and learning errors—essential elements for long-term student success.

A Lighter Backpack

In a long-forgotten television advertisement for spaghetti sauce, a series of people ask the question, "Does it have . . . ?" Through a dozen such inquiries, the answer is always, "It's in there!" So it is with students and their backpacks.

"Do you have your mathematics homework?"

"It's in there!"

"Do you have the letter from the principal to your parents?"

"It's in there!"

"Do you have the note from your teacher threatening a failing grade if you don't turn in more homework?"

"It's in there!"

"Do you have the hamster that Mr. Cleland said that he gave to you for safekeeping two days ago?"

"It's in there!"

My argument, based on many years of observing and carrying backpacks of progressively increasing weight, is that we use technology to capture the work that students do and use backpacks for the bare necessities—makeup, cell phones, and the stuff students don't want their parents to see. I'm sure the list is longer, but perhaps a better rule is what should *not* go into backpacks: academic work by parents that teachers, parents, and students must see and use in order to continue on a path of academic improvement.

When we are equipped with electronic gradebooks and digital education resources and software, such as electronic portfolios, backpacks should get lighter. Communication with parents does not depend on students digging materials out of a backpack but instead on direct communication between schools and parents. The statement, "It's in there!" applies to comprehensive databases and not antiquated student storage systems.

Collaborative Scoring of Anonymous Student Work

One of the least used and most promising uses of technology is the collaborative scoring of anonymous student work. Most teachers, particularly those who have suffered through graduate-level studies, understand that every assessment must be valid and reliable.

Validity is testing what we think we are testing, so conscientious mathematics teachers strive for validity by giving assessments that not only use story problems (a test of English and mathematics) but also problems involving only numbers and symbols (more likely a test of mathematics). Reliability is a test of consistency—will different evaluators examine the same piece of student work and come to similar results?

Two procedures are available to answer this question. The first procedure is for teachers to gather in a room, look at the same anonymous piece of student work, and then, working independently, assign a score to it. Then, the teachers share their scores and discuss the reasons behind their scoring differences. During this process, teachers may change their minds or, more likely, decide that the scoring rubric is insufficiently specific to come to a common conclusion. Once they decide they can change the scoring rubric to allow for greater specificity, the teachers quickly come to agreement, or at least a consensus, in which 80 percent or more agree on the final score.

The second procedure is to have assessment moderators compare their expert scores to those provided by the teachers. In this process, the quality of teacher assessment is not the result of collaboration or refined rubrics but rather the conformity of those scores with the moderators' judgments.

Live meetings like this have many advantages, including building collegiality among the group. Group members soon learn that the enemy is not one another; the enemy is ambiguity. As a group, they seek to improve the clarity and specificity of their scoring rubrics. This helps students obtain clear messages about their performance and helps teachers provide consistent feedback. However, group performance can become insular, and the impetus toward congeniality can dominate the necessity of collegiality.

Technology can play an especially powerful role in not only bringing together colleagues who are physically present but also in bringing together colleagues from around the world who can offer varied and valuable perspectives on the same student work, the same scoring rubric, and coming to a professional conclusion about the score students should receive. If your local colleagues believe that a piece of student work is a 3 on a four-point scale, but your colleagues in Shanghai and Finland mark it as a 2, then that is not necessarily an indication that your standards are too low. However, it is certainly an indication that the scoring rubric can benefit from additional specificity. If schools aspire to be world class, then they must follow the rhetoric with action, comparing the quality of student work with examples from Singapore, South Korea, Ontario, Finland, or other nations to which your school system would like to be compared. Skype, GoToMeeting, and other emerging (and free) global communication systems make collaboration and consistency accessible to every school.

Parent Engagement With Electronic Gradebooks

As noted earlier, one of the most powerful capabilities of electronic gradebooks is enhanced communication between the school and parents. There is a stark difference between parent compliance and parent engagement when it comes to electronic gradebooks. At the most facile level, electronic monitoring becomes the source of an unproductive and eternal argument.

"Did you turn in your homework?"

"Yes, I did."

"No, you didn't."

"Yes, I did."

"I just checked online, and it says that you didn't turn in the homework."

"That just means that the teacher hasn't entered it in the database—I DID turn it in!"

"No, you didn't!"

"Yes, I did!"

These are not the conversations that technology promoters had in mind when they assumed that parental access to report card information would lead parents to have deep discussions about student achievement. At their very best, electronic grading systems provide students, teachers, and parents with an early warning system to prevent student failure. With or without technology, teachers often know, with stunning degrees of accuracy, which students will fail and which students will succeed. Students themselves also make accurate predictions (Hattie, 2012).

But research on teacher and student expectations casts a backward glance on the relationship between personal expectations and student results. Used effectively, electronic gradebooks can break the cycle of low expectations followed by low results. At very narrow intervals, perhaps one week—certainly no more than two weeks—teachers should be able to ask, "Who is in danger of failing?" and more importantly, "What interventions can we use right now to avoid failure?"

If the problem is homework, then the appropriate response might be some of the interventions described in earlier chapters, such the quiet table, coach's corner, or other methods designed to give students time to get back on track. To be clear, the response to missing homework is neither excuses nor ignoring the challenge that practice is essential but rather finding opportunities for practice—what homework should really be—in nontraditional settings. After all, teachers don't send home the basketball team with basketballs in their backpacks, instructing players to respond to problems about the theory of basketball. The players practice together, guided by a coach and supported by one another. This is precisely what band members, cheerleaders, and drama club members do outside of school. They practice, with support of teachers and fellow students.

Therefore, if a teacher in any subject knows two weeks into the school term that a student needs more practice—as evidenced by poor homework performance—the answer must not be a letter containing threats of failure but rather the creation of a different setting for practice. In almost every school, we know how to do this—the only question is whether we are willing to learn from our colleagues and take the actions required, informed by technology resources, to get the maximum number of students back on track.

In sum, technology is nothing but a tool, but it is a tool with widely varying applications. That tool can be like a hammer—useful but barely changed from prehistoric times. Or, the tool can be like fire—starting out as a source of heat and eventually becoming the source of energy and power to fuel modern civilization. Technology can lead to mind-numbing experiences or mind-expanding experiences, as students discover new and varied opportunities for collaboration, creativity, and communication.

Effective use of technology can enhance student and teacher collaboration on a global scale, including exchanging emails and instant messages and live video conversations. Students can model complex mathematical and scientific projects and immediately get feedback on their performance. With the click of a mouse, they can compare their writing and life experiences to their peers' from around the world. Teachers can share lessons, assessments, and teaching strategies across districts, states, and continents. By collaborating on a larger scale, students and teachers no longer provide evidence of these successes with a few local anecdotes but with a large body of international evidence.

Teachers can use technology in mind-numbingly simple ways—entering data in a gradebook with the same results that they have had for decades. Or, they can use technology to motivate, encourage, and engage students, parents, and colleagues to inspire a new generation of innovative thinkers.

INSPIRING CHANGE IN GRADING POLICIES

The acid test for any grading policy is the degree to which it is working. By *working*, I mean whether students, teachers, and parents can use the feedback from the grading policy to improve performance. Students in the early primary grades can, when given the opportunity, respond to the question, "What do you think you need to do to get better?" Those students whose teachers have employed standards-based assessment systems in student-accessible language can say with confidence, "I only got a 2, because I forgot to . . ." and quickly add, "But next time, I'm going to get a 3, because I will . . ." The use of numbers, letters, or words is immaterial in this example. What is most important, when evaluating grading systems against the standard of effectiveness, is that students use the feedback to improve their performance. In order to achieve these objectives, grading systems must be FAST—fair, accurate, specific, and timely.

While almost all schools have discussed grading policy reforms, those that succeed in implementing effective change follow some distinctive and consistent patterns. Change leaders in those schools:

- Engage in extensive community dialogue
- Use grading as a tool for improved student learning
- Tolerate dissent (and don't let it intimidate them)
- Demonstrate effective change with evidence of improved student success

Engage in Extensive Community Dialogue

Change leaders do not merely announce a change in grading policies but engage in extensive community dialogue. Leaders from Waukesha, Wisconsin, and Wamego, Kansas, used a careful process of deliberate, deep, and broad engagement of stakeholders, including students, parents, school board members, union leaders, and community members. They documented their own best practices and carefully considered the best available evidence from national and international sources. Their changes in grading policies, while not universally popular, were the subject of extensive collaboration and dialogue. For example, changing from a one hundred–point scale to a four-point scale and changing from using the average to an assessment of student proficiency at the end of the marking period can have a significant and positive impact on student success. These relatively simple changes, however, are fraught with controversy. This is why policy changes without extensive and meaningful dialogue with parents, community members, and policymakers are ineffective.

Use Grading as a Tool for Improved Student Learning

Change leaders of successful grading policies embrace a clear set of principles about the fundamental purposes of grading as a tool for improved student learning. They reject grading as a form of punishment and manipulation and embrace it as a means of communication and feedback. Their purpose is neither to sort students nor to judge them but to help them become more successful.

Tolerate Dissent

Change leaders are tolerant of dissent, but it does not intimidate them. They do not expect every conversation to be easy or for strong emotions not to accompany viewpoints. They recognize that existing grading policies have strong advocates, not because those advocates are bad people, but because they care deeply about their profession and practice. Both sides emerge from these difficult conversations because they recognize that people can differ on the issues and nevertheless share a passionate commitment to students.

Demonstrate Effective Change With Improved Student Success

Most importantly, change leaders who modify grading policies demonstrate the effectiveness of these changes with improved student success. They win over skeptics not with rhetoric but with results. When their grading policies improve, their failure rates decline. When failures decline, discipline and morale improve. When fewer resources are diverted to course repetition and student remediation, more resources are available for activities that engage the interest and excitement of students and teachers alike. Ultimately, their actions are not based on authority or policy but on impact.

Although this book offers examples of effective grading practices, these are meant to be useful strategies for starting a conversation about the grading practices in your school and community. The rule should be "principles before policies." Nearly all participants in a discussion of grading practices and policies can agree that grading should be fair—students with the same proficiency should receive the same grade. Surely we can find common ground that grades should be accurate—based not on nonacademic matters but on academic work. Students and parents are happiest when grades are specific—that is, students know precisely what they must do in order to improve their performance. And finally, grades and all other kinds of feedback are most effective when they are timely.

I hope this book inspires many productive and enlightening conversations on this vitally important topic, and as a result, promotes the implementation of grading practices and policies that provide students with the foundation they need to succeed both in school and in life.

Appendix

REPRODUCIBLES

Distortions in Grading
Through the Use of Zero Points

Use these graphs to understand how distortions in grading arise by using the 0 for missing work. Mark the point value for missing work on each graph, and look at the relative weight of the grade in each case.

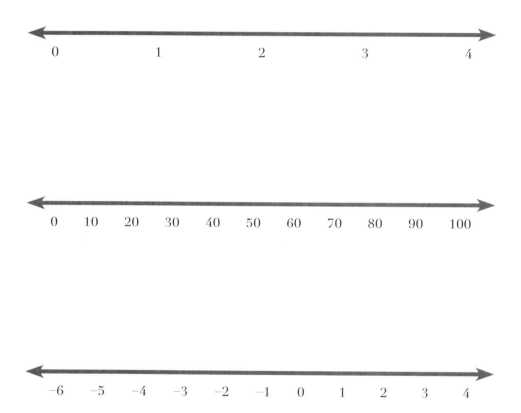

Equity in Grading Self-Assessment

The purpose of this form is to help teachers and administrators explore the relationship between student grades, academic performance, and nonacademic factors. This inquiry may be helpful in improving the equity of your assessment and grading practices. Although designed for classroom use, it can be modified for use by an entire school or school system.

1. Treasure Hunt: Find the As

Look at the most recent report cards, and enter in the table the names and profiles of students who earned As or, if you use a different terminology for reporting student results, the highest available mark.

Name	Gender	Low Income?	Ethnic Minority?	Language Minority?

What do you notice about the profile of your A students? What demographic characteristics do they have in common?

2. Search and Rescue Mission: Find the Ds and Fs

Look at the most recent report cards, and enter in the table the names and profiles of students who earned Ds and Fs or, if you use a different terminology for reporting student results, the lowest available marks.

Name	Gender	Low Income?	Ethnic Minority?	Language Minority?

What do you notice about the profile of your lowest-performing students? What demographic characteristics do they have in common?

3. High Grades and Low Achievement

Look at your most recent external assessment data. These might be state or provincial tests, district tests, or any other indicator outside of regular classroom work. Find the students who were not proficient on these tests but had good grades in your class—Bs and As or comparable marks in a nonletter grading system. Record their profiles in the table.

Name	Gender	Low Income?	Ethnic Minority?	Language Minority?

What do you notice about the profile of your students with high grades and low achievement? What demographic characteristics do they have in common?

4. Low Grades and High Achievement

Refer to your most recent external assessments, and find the students who scored well but nevertheless have low grades—Ds and Fs or comparable marks in your system. Record their profiles in the table.

Name	Gender	Low Income?	Ethnic Minority?	Language Minority?

What do you notice about the profiles of your students with low grades and high achievement? What demographic characteristics do they have in common?

Elements of Grading, Second Edition © 2016 Solution Tree Press • solution-tree.com
Visit **go.solution-tree.com/assessment** to download this page.

Sample Grading Policy

AIS-R Assessment, Evaluation, and Reporting

1. Assessment Philosophy

Assessment is the systematic process of gathering a variety of information over time, demonstrating what students know and can do, as well as what they need to know. The role of assessment is to provide meaningful feedback for improving both student learning and instructional practice.

2. Core Beliefs

- The primary purpose of assessment is to improve learning.

- Assessment provides the most accurate profile of a student's abilities. A variety of assessment tools must be used to ensure this.

- Assessment evaluates the process as well as the products of learning.

- To assess performance and progress, it is critical to develop standards-based criteria based on benchmarks.

- Assessment indicates if the student has learned.

- Assessment provides an opportunity for the teacher to reflect on his/her instructional effectiveness.

- External, standardized assessment has a role in curriculum revision.

- Self-assessment provides an opportunity for students to reflect on and evaluate their performance.

Performance is evaluated from the assessment information collected.

Evaluation is the process by which a teacher makes sense of all the information collected, determining whether standards of achievement have been attained. Just as important is the evaluation of the effectiveness of the instructional program delivered.

Reporting is the process by which we communicate learning and achievement on a systematic basis to students and parents.

3. Reporting and Parent Conferences

Communicating with parents is an essential part of the student-parent-teacher partnership. Teachers continually communicate student progress both formally and informally.

ES report cards *are issued to all students three times a year at the end of each trimester period in December, March, and June.*

MS/HS report cards *are issued to all students four times a year at the end of each nine-week period in November, January, April, and June.*

- **Elementary School:** Report cards demonstrate the academic progress students are making in the form of narrative comments and accompanying marks. All elementary school reports are paperless and available via Skyward.

- **Middle School:** Report cards demonstrate the academic progress students are making in their courses in the form of written comments and accompanying grades. Student transcripts show only letter grades at the end of each semester. All student reports are available on Family Access in Skyward.

- **High School:** All high school report cards are paperless. Parents will be notified when to log on to Family Access at the end of each quarter in order to check their child's academic progress, effort, and grade point average. Absences and tardies are also noted.

Progress Reports *are intended to promote communication that allows parents, students, and teachers to develop an intervention strategy for a struggling student or to provide positive feedback related to student performance, attitude, or contributions to the classroom or school.*

- **Elementary School:** Progress reports may be sent home mid-trimester when there is a concern about a student's progress, a student's work is failing, or when there has been exceptional progress. All elementary students will receive a progress report during the first trimester. No student should be awarded a minimal achievement mark in any subject on the report card unless parents have been notified in advance that the student's work has been unsatisfactory. Some teachers send progress reports to celebrate students' learning.

- **Middle School:** The middle school designates a progress report period in the middle of each quarter. A notice is sent home to parents to encourage them to check their child's progress in Skyward. Teachers may also include it in the gradebook at this time. Progress reports may be sent home at any time, especially when there is a concern about a student's progress, a student's work is failing, or when there has been exceptional progress.

- **High School:** The high school designates a progress report period in the middle of each quarter. A notice is sent home to parents to encourage them to check their child's progress in Skyward. Teachers may also include it in the gradebook at this time. Progress reports may be sent home at any time, especially when there is a concern about a student's progress, a student's work is failing, or when there has been exceptional progress.

Parent Conferences are held twice a year in November and February. At these conferences, report cards and student progress are reviewed by the teacher and parents. Conferences between parents and teachers are very helpful in creating an understanding with regard to educational goals and objectives, solving problem situations, developing plans for helping students at home, and informing parents of student progress.

- **Elementary School:** Specially arranged conferences between parents and teachers are very helpful in creating an understanding with regard to educational goals and objectives, solving problem situations, developing plans for helping students at home, and informing parents of student progress. Conferences may be scheduled at the request of the parents, teachers, counselors, or administrators.

- **Middle School:** Parents are encouraged to make appointments for conferences with staff members at any time during the school year. Parents are encouraged to request conferences periodically, especially if problems are indicated.

- **High School:** Parents are encouraged to make appointments for conferences with staff members at any time during the school year. Teachers may occasionally wish to speak with parents by telephone or in person, especially when circumstances require discussion or clarification. Students on Academic Probation or Conditional Acceptance are required to attend conferences with their parents.

4. Grading and Reporting

Each division has developed common agreements on grading and reporting that best support student learning at each level.

Elementary School:

Understandings:

- The report is separated into three parts: Subject, Social Skills, and Work Study Skills (I am an AIS-R EAGLE).

- Behaviors are only reflected in Oral Communication, Social Skills, and Study Skills (I am an AIS-R EAGLE).

- Unless specifically tied to a standard, the following behaviors will not be evaluated, scored, and recorded as part of a student's subject score:

  1. Effort

  2. Personal organization

  3. Attendance

  4. Participation

2014–2015 Agreements:

- To use evidence from individual achievement only

- To measure student performance against preset standards (such as rubric indicators)

- To use only summative evidence for reporting and formative evidence to inform our instruction

- That learning is developmental and we use the most recent assessment to reflect learning for reporting

- To determine if a child has met the standard in reading, we use the mode when communicating the results as evidenced by the Individual Profile of Progress

- To provide students with opportunities to self-assess and reflect on their learning and progress for diagnostic and formative purposes

- To follow the AIS-R Elementary School Report Card Guidelines

- To follow the AIS-R Elementary School Reading Assessment and Reporting Guidelines http://blogs.ais-r.edu.sa/espln/files/2013/06/AIS-R-ES-Report-Card-Guidelines.pdf

Homework Guidelines:

- HW is not mandatory.

- HW targets a student's independent level and is therefore differentiated. At no time should all students be completing the same HW, at the same time, in the same way (unless evidenced by a preassessment or formative assessment). "To ensure homework is doable, teachers must differentiate assignments so they are at the appropriate level of difficulty for individual students" (Tomlinson, 2008). How to differentiate? Consider amount, time, type, competence, efficiency, choice, and personal relevance.

- When assigned, the student(s) must be given feedback on their HW performance. HW is formative and does not factor into a student's report card.

- When assigned, HW must be communicated with the respective parents/families (for example, email, blog post, assignment notebook) and not exceed thirty minutes for grades 1–3 and forty-five minutes for grades 4–5.

Middle School:

Understandings:

- The report card is separated into two parts: Academics and Commitment to Learning.

- Reporting on Commitment to Learning is done using the following categories:

1. Organization
2. Work habits
3. Works independently
4. Initiative
5. Teamwork
6. Behavior

- Commitment to Learning rubrics with more specific descriptors are provided to students and parents (see Appendix C).
- The following labels are used for reporting behaviors: *Rarely, Sometimes, Usually,* and *Consistently Observed.*

2014–2015 Agreements:

Late Work Policy:

Late work can be submitted up until the final summative assessment for any given unit. Once a unit is complete, late work is not accepted unless the late work in question happens to be part or all of the final summative assessment, such as a project or a presentation. In the case of late work being a final assessment, it is up to the discretion of each individual teacher as to how the work is accepted.

Retake Policy:

All formative assessments and work must be complete prior to a student being eligible for a retake on a summative assessment. If a student qualifies for a retake, the teacher makes a determination about the student being allowed a retake based on factors that are included in the rubrics and unit outlines for each particular class.

Homework Policy:

Will not count homework as part of the grade. It will be addressed in the Commitment to Learning section of the report card.

High School:

Understandings:

- Unless specifically tied to a standard, the following behaviors will not be evaluated, scored, and recorded as part of a student's academic grade:

    1. Effort

    2. Personal organization

    3. Punctuality

    4. Attendance

    5. Participation

- Each department has aligned summative assessments/products with IB Diploma Programme assessment practices, criteria, and rubrics.

- Students will not receive marks for formative assessments/development tasks, which are designed to enable students to receive feedback. The purpose of the feedback is to enable students to succeed better on the summative performances of understanding, whatever form they might take.

2014–2015 Agreements:

All Non-IB Courses (Grades 9 and 10 and Electives):

- Development tasks: For practice during the learning process, gives teacher feedback on what students know; gives students feedback on what they still need to learn; does not "count"

- Products: For real at the end of the learning process, gives teachers and students feedback on what was learned against the standards/benchmarks; "counts"

- Guidelines to follow:

    - Minimum of two development tasks prior to a product

    - Minimum of five products per semester (minimum of two per quarter)

    - Product tasks should be completed in class

    - Manila folder of work for each student to track growth and to be used at grading time (benchmark/diagnostic, choice developmental and all products)

All IB Courses:

- Summative: High-stakes assessments; "counts"

- Formative: For practice, low-stakes assessment; "counts" *(This definition is different than in other divisions due to tradition; in 2016–17, this category will be eliminated.)*

- Development tasks: For practice during the learning process, gives teacher feedback on what students know; gives students feedback on what they still need to learn; does not "count"

- Guidelines to follow:

  - Development tasks with a value of 0

  - Summative with a minimum value of 60 percent— high stakes (TBD by department)

  - Formative with a maximum value of 20 percent— low stakes (TBD by department)

  - Exams with a value of 20 percent

  - No completion grades for homework

  - Point value per task is up to teacher (10 points versus 200 points)

  - Additional column for an IB score (according to AIS-R scale; see Appendix B)

  - Optional "best fit grade"

Late Work Policy:

- Students are expected to submit assignments before the designated deadlines. Meeting deadlines requires responsibility, and students should manage their time and prioritize so deadlines are successfully met. To support students' efforts in meeting this expectation, teachers shall (a) announce deadlines in advance, (b) provide sufficient time as determined by their professional judgment, and (c) post assignments and their deadlines on Moodle.

- Students who do not submit assignments on time will attend the after-school Student Success Center (SSC) for Work Completion until the assignment is completed. If the work

Elements of Grading, Second Edition © 2016 Solution Tree Press • solution-tree.com
Visit **go.solution-tree.com/assessment** to download this page.

is not finished after one week, the student will also attend Saturday School from 8:00 a.m.–12:00 p.m. If the work is still incomplete, the student will receive a 0 on the assignment.

- Students who are repeatedly late with assignments will meet with the Dean of Students and their parents to discuss the need to improve work habits to be successful as an AIS-R EAGLE.

Academic Honesty Policy:

- All summative assessments that are not tests and examinations are submitted through Turnitin.com. Extended Essay drafts are submitted through the Turnitin.com link on Managebac.

- AIS-R expects and requires that students will uphold the highest standards of ethics and academic excellence. The Academic Honesty Policy represents our effort to guarantee that students are committed to building and maintaining a learning community of the highest integrity by carrying out academic tasks with honesty in all situations.

- Definition: *Academic dishonesty includes, but is not limited to, the following.*

  - Plagiarism (using someone else's ideas or words without giving credit to that person, including direct quotes, paraphrasing, or summarizing)

  - Copying by any means other students' homework (Students who are observed in common areas looking at their own and another student's lab notebook, worksheet, or any other homework assignment would be assumed to be in violation of this rule, regardless of the exact wording of their work. Equally, students submitting assignments with identical phrases in free-response sections would be assumed to have violated the policy.)

  - Allowing one's homework to be copied (In this regard, all homework is considered individual work unless otherwise stated by the teacher. As such, no student should physically give his or her homework to another student. If copying occurs, it will be presumed that the student who gave his or her homework to the copying student allowed the homework to be copied.)

- Using written formulas, hidden reference sheets, notes, codes, or key words on one's person or objects for use on any test, quiz, presentation, or assignment without prior permission from the teacher; also, carrying such materials with the intention of using them on a test or exam

- Looking at another student's test or quiz during its administration or using programmed material in watches, calculators, phones, MP3 players, or computer programs without permission from the teacher

- Giving answers or questions to another student during or after a test or quiz; receiving answers or questions from a student who is taking or has already taken a test or quiz (Students engaged in any form of unauthorized communication while in the possession of a test or quiz may be presumed to be in violation of this rule.)

- Using the Internet, laptop computers, text messaging, phone cameras, MP3 players, or other modern technology to plagiarize, copy, or share work with another student (including but not limited to copying and pasting, in whole or in part, material from the Internet; purchasing material from the Internet to be submitted as one's own work; using a translation program for a world language class; presenting lab data found on the Internet as one's original work; or using email to share individual homework assignments)

- Taking credit for work done by someone else (for example, family members or tutors), including submitting rough drafts or similar work created by another person

- Presenting invented data (for example, lab results for lab activities that have not actually been conducted), information, or cited sources (in a bibliography) as authentic

- Any deceitful means used on a test, quiz, or assignment, including but not limited to stealing electronic or paper copies of tests from teachers' classrooms or computers; receiving copies of tests, quizzes, or assignments from students who took the class in previous years;

possessing unauthorized teachers' materials; taking credit for work not completed (as in group assignments); or submitting the same assignment for credit in multiple classes without teachers' permission

- Any other behavior that could be reasonably construed as academic dishonesty, including class-specific expectations explained in teachers' syllabi

Note: On cooperative work: All written work is individual work unless otherwise stated by the classroom teacher. Although it is acceptable to talk with classmates, friends, and family members about what you are studying and thinking, do not compose written work collaboratively, and make sure that written work you submit for credit is presented entirely in your own words when quotation marks are not used.

Consequences for Acts of Academic Dishonesty

All academic honesty violations will be reported to the High School Leadership Team and counseling office. A record of the violation will be put in the student's permanent file. In cases of significant or repeated offenses, American International School of Riyadh will report acts of Academic Dishonesty to college admission officers.

First offense at AIS-R:

1. Student will receive a 0 for the assignment, test, quiz, project, or exam.

2. Student will be required to meet with the Principal and/ or Assistant Principal or Dean of Students to discuss the importance of academic integrity.

3. Student's parents will be informed of the violation.

4. Student will receive an after-school detention.

Second offense at AIS-R:

1. Student will receive a 0 for the assignment, test, quiz, project, or exam and may receive a failing grade in the class where the violation occurred.

2. Student's parents will be informed of the violation.

3. Student will be required to meet with the Principal and/ or Assistant Principal or Dean of Students to discuss the importance of academic integrity.

4. Student will receive Saturday School Detention.

Third offense at AIS-R:

1. Student will be subject to receive a failing grade in the class where the violation occurred.

2. Student's parents will be informed of the violation.

3. Student will be required to meet with the Principal and their parents to discuss the importance of academic integrity.

4. Student will be suspended from all sports and extracurricular activities for the duration of the season or quarter.

5. Student will receive a two-day, out-of-school suspension from school.

Additional offenses at AIS-R:

Additional offenses will result in expulsion from the American International School.

Note: If a student facing expulsion for an academic honesty violation has had no acts of academic dishonesty for at least one full calendar year, the school may choose, at the Principal's discretion, to allow the student to present information to support his or her ability to continue attending school and/or school-related events.

Academic Dishonesty and IB

It is the responsibility of AIS-R as an IB World School to uphold the integrity of all IB Examinations and Internal Assessments (IAs). As such, our academic honesty policy is in line with the IB expectations of and requirements for us as an IB World School. Our policy is clear and has straightforward procedures and penalties. It is in line with the IB General Regulation's expectations.

The IB Learner Profile is embedded into AIS-R's daily life and is therefore, along with our AIS-R's EAGLE Honor Code, the cornerstone of this policy. Further guidance comes from the IB Publication's *Academic*

Honesty: Guidance for Schools (September 2003). In developing AIS-R's Academic Honesty Policy, we encourage our students to be:

- Inquirers, who acquire the skills necessary to conduct inquiry and research

- Knowledgeable, and explore concepts, ideas, and issues

- Principled, and act with integrity and honesty, taking responsibility for their own actions

- Open-minded, and accustomed to seeking and evaluating a range of points of view

- Risk takers, who are brave and articulate in defending their beliefs

These qualities, when applied to learning and student work, will establish skills and behavior that support good practices to be found in the classroom, used for homework, and continued to examination level. These good practices are expected to be introduced, modeled, and used throughout the school. These practices are also clearly articulated in our Eagle Honor Code.

5. Gathering Evidence and Information (See Appendix D for division-specific information.)

Diagnostic Assessment occurs at the beginning of the teaching/learning cycle. This type of assessment will provide the teacher with an understanding of the prior knowledge and skills a student brings to a unit, as well as the strengths and specific learning needs of an individual or groups of students in relation to the expectations that will be taught.

Self-Assessment promotes learning by:

- Giving learners training in evaluation, which results in benefits to the learning process

- Giving both students and teachers a raised level of awareness of perceived levels of abilities

- Encouraging learners to look at course content in a more discerning way

Formative Assessments are assessments FOR learning. It is ongoing and provides evidence of and for progression in learning. It supports learning through identifying difficulties, providing feedback, and diagnosing future learning priorities for the student and teacher.

Summative Assessments are assessments OF learning. It is used mainly to measure performance and summarizes the development of learners at a particular time. It is carried out at the end of a period of learning. It is a final judgment of learning.

Common Assessments ensure consistency between classrooms. They allow teachers to evaluate how well their students are doing relative to the selected standards not only in their classrooms but also in other grade-level classrooms/subjects. These benchmark assessments use standardized administration and scoring procedures to help maintain validity, reliability, and fairness. They provide valuable information for classroom practice and grade-level, divisional, and schoolwide decision making, including accreditation.

External Assessments inform us on how students perform individually, as a class, and as a grade level, in relation to other students. Since the same test is given to a large number of students throughout the world, the results give us a common yardstick or "standard" of measure to determine whether school programs are succeeding or a snapshot of the skills and abilities of district students.

6. Roles and Responsibilities of Assessment, Evaluation, and Reporting of Data in Order to Improve Learning

The role of assessment is to provide meaningful feedback for improving both student learning and instructional practice. Assessment results serve as one of the many sources of data gathered and analyzed to improve the school's programs.

All members of the school community play an integral role in improving student learning.

It is the responsibility of the Superintendent and Learning Office to:

- Review, monitor, and evaluate all aspects of the school's assessment practices within the context of the whole school development plan and self-evaluation

- Coordinate the collection and analysis of schoolwide assessment data

- Use assessment data in the curriculum review process

- Use assessment data in planning professional learning opportunities for faculty

- Ensure that accreditation standards are being articulated, met, and maintained

It is the responsibility of the Principals and Assistant Principals to:

- Apply and embed the principles of the school's assessment practices within their own division

- Support their staff in the use of assessment data to inform teaching and learning

- Supervise the grading and reporting process at their division

- Liaise with teachers regarding individual pupil performance as required

- Ensure that accreditation standards are being articulated, met, and maintained

It is the responsibility of the Heads of Department/Team Leaders to:

- Work with their department to embed the principles of the school's assessment practices

- Work with their department to establish common assessment practices

- Gather and analyze data from common assessments for the purpose of program improvement

- Ensure that accreditation standards are being articulated, met, and maintained

It is the responsibility of the Counselors to:

- Coordinate the external examinations for their division
- Liaise with teachers regarding individual pupil performance as required

It is the responsibility of the Teachers to:

- Implement and evaluate departmental/whole school practices on assessment, evaluation, and reporting
- Compile and maintain individual student records
- Report to students, parents, and supervisors on individual student progress
- Liaise with teaching teams regarding individual student support as required
- Ensure that accreditation standards are being articulated, met, and maintained

It is the responsibility of the Parents to:

- Communicate regularly with teachers
- Attend parent-teacher conferences
- Support their child's learning

It is the responsibility of the Students to:

- Be fully prepared for assessments
- Perform at their highest level on assessments
- Keep parents informed of their level of performance

*Based on *The School Curriculum: Design and Review (New Zealand Ministry of Education).*

Appendix A

AIS-R Assessment Tools

Type	Description	Examples
Selected Response	Students must recognize and select the correct answer from a preset list of responses. Answer can be scored as correct or incorrect.	True/false, multiple choice, matching, fill in the blank
Constructed Response	Students create their own response within a limited framework (visual, written, or oral) by retrieving information, organizing it in a logical manner, and explaining their logic (visual, written, or oral).	Short answer, vocabulary quiz, computation problems, compare, classify, create metaphors or analogies, analyze errors
Essay (Academic Prompt)	Written work on a topic, question, or issue that requires students to share and/or react to information with no particular audience	Narrative, academic writing, report, journal, logs
School Product or Performance	Tasks that require students to create or do something in the school context	Create a model, draw a diagram, create a portfolio, labs
Oral Responses and Oral Reports	Tasks that involves attention to the needs of the audience, careful planning, and attention to delivery	Present a report; share a model, diagram, or portfolio; have an impromptu discussion with others students and/or the teacher
Contextualized Task (Including Oral Responses or Reports)	Tasks that require students to make or do something involving attention to the needs of the audience or purpose, careful planning, and attention to delivery (simulated or real); this is also sometimes referred to as Authentic Assessment	Write an editorial for a newspaper; make a speech at a town meeting; construct a model for an exhibition; present a report; share a model, diagram, or portfolio; have an impromptu discussion with others students and/or the teacher

Type	Description	Examples
Observation Tools	Tools designed to collect evidence of work processes and understanding "of the moment"	Checklist of behavior, anecdotal records

*Based on the research of Bambi Betts (2008) and Robert Marzano (2008).

Appendix B

Achievement Charts

Elementary School

Elementary report cards include a narrative description of the student's growth and content area assessment.

Early childhood education (KG2–grade 2) content area assessments use the following grading scheme:

Grading Scheme	Definition
CD	I can: Student consistently demonstrates understanding of concepts, content, and skills at grade level at the time of the report card.
DS	I am learning: Student is developing steadily and demonstrates some understanding—with support—of concepts, content, and skills at grade level at the time of the report card.
ES	I need more time: Student is in the early stage and requires significant support to understand concepts, content, and skills at the time of the report card.
ESL	English as a second language
NA	Not assessed at this time

Upper elementary school (grades 3–5) content area assessments use the following grading scheme:

Grading Scheme	Definition
CD	Consistently displayed: Student consistently meets all grade-level expectations independently.
DE	Developing as expected: Student meets most grade-level expectations independently.
DS	Developing steadily: Student meets most grade-level expectations and requires added support.
ES	Early stages: Student is not yet meeting grade-level expectations and requires significant support.
ESL	English as a second language
NA	Not assessed at this time

K–5 ES Reading

Reading on the ES report card is standards based.

The Grading Scheme includes "Approaches Learning Goal" or "Meets Learning Goal." The Learning Goals are outlined as follows.

1. Reading: Informational Text

   - Reads grade-level text with purpose and understanding
   - Applies reading skills at independent reading level

2. Reading: Literature

   - Reads grade-level text with purpose and understanding
   - Applies reading skills at independent reading level

Middle School

Middle school report cards include course-specific letter grades and comments.

Course-specific letter grades are based on the following scheme:

Grade/ Percent	Grade/ Percent	Grade/ Percent	Grade/ Percent	Grade/ Percent	Grade/ Percent	Grade/ Percent	Grade/ Percent
A+	97 or above	B+	87–89	C+	77–79	D+	67–69
A	93–96	B	83–86	C	73–76	D	63–66
A–	90–92	B–	80–82	C–	70–72	D–	60–62
						F	50–59

I – The student submits incomplete work.

P – The student does his or her work satisfactorily. He or she is demonstrating achievement.

N – The student does not receive a grade because he or she did not meet the minimum number of days required "in attendance."

High School

High school report cards include course-specific letter grades and comments.

Course-specific letter grades are based on the following scheme:

Grade	Percent	GPA	Grade	Percent	GPA
A+	97 or above	4.3	C+	77–79	2.3
			C	73–76	2.0
A	93–96	4.0	C–	70–72	1.7
A–	90–92	3.7	D+	67–69	1.3
B+	87–89	3.3	D	63–66	1.0
B	83–86	3.0	D–	60–62	0.7
B–	80–82	2.7	F	59 or below	0

*Grade point average calculated for college applications is derived from semester grades of ALL classes taken at AIS-R's high school. IB Higher Level II courses are weighted by an additional .3 on grades of B+ or higher.

IB Conversion Chart

IB course grades are converted into percentages on the AIS-R report cards according to the following chart.

IB Grades	IB Scale	AIS-R Letter Grade	AIS-R Percentage Equivalent
7	Excellent	A+	97–100
		A	93–96
6	Very Good	A–	90–92
		B+	87–89
5	Good	B	83–86
		B–	80–82
4	Satisfactory	C+	77–79
		C	73–76
3	Mediocre	C–	70–72
		D+	67–69
2	Poor	D	63–66
		D–	60–62
1		F	0–59

Appendix C

Middle School Commitment to Learning

Organization (Time, Material, and Information Management)

Criteria	Rarely	Sometimes	Usually	Consistently
Notes are in order and complete.	Notes are often out of order and/or incomplete.	Notes are more often than not in order or complete.	Notes are usually in order and complete.	Notes are consistently in order and complete.

Criteria	Rarely	Sometimes	Usually	Consistently
Uses planners or agendas to track deadlines or tasks	Use of organizational tools is ineffective	Use of organizational tools is moderately effective	Use of organizational tools is effective	Use of organizational tools is highly effective
Makes a work plan of action (time management)	Makes a work plan only with assistance or not at all	Makes a work plan sometimes or with frequent assistance	Makes a work plan most of the time or with occasional assistance	Always makes a work plan independently
Changes work plan when necessary	Shows little awareness of need to revise work plan, or makes changes only with assistance	Shows some awareness of need to revise work plan, or makes changes with some assistance	Shows good awareness of need to revise work plan, or makes changes with little assistance	Revises work plan when needed and independently

Work Habits (Responsibility, Classwork, Homework)

Criteria	Rarely	Sometimes	Usually	Consistently
Brings own supplies and book to class	Rarely brings necessary materials	Sometimes brings necessary materials	Almost always brings necessary materials	Always brings necessary materials
Completes/ submits work on time	Rarely completes or submits work on time	Sometimes completes or submits work on time	Frequently completes or submits work on time	Consistently completes or submits work on time
Makes an effort to complete classwork	Effort put into work is ineffective	Effort put into work is moderately effective	Effort put into work is effective	Effort put into work is highly effective

Criteria	Rarely	Sometimes	Usually	Consistently
Revises work before submitting	Proofreads work for content or errors ineffectively	Proofreads work for content or errors with moderate effectiveness	Proofreads work for content or errors effectively	Verifies and reviews work for content or errors in a highly effective manner
Follows safety rules	Consistently needs reminding of safety issues	Sometimes needs reminding of safety issues	Follows safety practices in the classroom	Follows and encourages safe classroom practices

Behavior (Respectful, Follows Rules, Takes Responsibility)

Criteria	Rarely	Sometimes	Usually	Consistently
Treats teachers, classmates, and self with respect	Rarely treats teachers, classmates, and/or self with respect	Sometimes treats teachers, classmates, and/or self with respect	Usually treats teachers, classmates, and/or self with respect	Consistently treats teachers, classmates, and/or self with respect
Respects and follows classroom and school rules	Rarely respects and follows classroom and school rules	Sometimes respects and follows classroom and school rules	Usually respects and follows classroom and school rules	Consistently respects and follows classroom and school rules
Is honest and trustworthy	Is rarely honest and trustworthy	Is sometimes honest and trustworthy	Is usually honest and trustworthy	Is consistently honest and trustworthy
Takes responsibility for own actions and work	Rarely takes responsibility for own actions and work	Sometimes takes responsibility for own actions and work	Usually takes responsibility for own actions and work	Consistently takes responsibility for own actions and work

Criteria	Rarely	Sometimes	Usually	Consistently
Refrains from physical and verbal abuse	Rarely refrains from physical and verbal abuse	Sometimes refrains from physical and verbal abuse	Usually refrains from physical and verbal abuse	Consistently refrains from physical and verbal abuse

Works Independently (Self-Direction, Persistence)

Criteria	Rarely	Sometimes	Usually	Consistently
Is a self-directed learner	Directs own learning only with assistance	Directs own learning with prompting	Directs own learning with minimal prompting	Directs own learning and generates own ideas
Follows instructions	Rarely follows instructions properly	Sometimes follows instructions properly	Usually follows instructions properly	Always follows instructions properly
Is willing to work	Requires constant encouragement to work	Needs encouragement to work	May need some encouragement to work	Requires little to no encouragement to work
Uses time wisely (in class or elsewhere)	Use of class time is ineffective	Use of class time is moderately effective	Use of class time is effective	Use of class time is highly effective
Perseveres when presented with a challenge	Rarely perseveres when presented with a challenge	Sometimes perseveres when presented with a challenge	Usually perseveres when presented with a challenge	Consistently perseveres when presented with a challenge

Initiative (Approach to Learning, Resourcefulness)

Criteria	Rarely	Sometimes	Usually	Consistently
Arrives to class on time	Rarely arrives to class on time	Sometimes arrives to class on time	Usually arrives to class on time	Consistently arrives to class on time
Gets to work	Rarely begins work without prompting	Sometimes begins work without prompting	Usually begins work without prompting	Consistently begins work without prompting
Asks for help or direction when needed	Request(s) for help or direction is ineffective	Request(s) for help or direction is moderately effective	Request(s) for help or direction is effective	Request(s) for help or direction is highly effective
Offers to help others appropriately	Rarely offers help	Sometimes offers help	Often offers help	Consistently offers help
Uses outside resources to support learning	Uses outside resources for learning ineffectively	Uses outside resources for learning with moderate effectiveness	Finds and uses some outside resources effectively	Incorporates a variety of resources in a highly effective manner

Teamwork (Cooperation, Responsibility, Roles)

Criteria	Rarely	Sometimes	Usually	Consistently
Listens to other people's opinions	Rarely listens passively or actively	Sometimes listens passively and actively by paraphrasing for accuracy	Often listens passively and actively by paraphrasing for accuracy	Regularly listens passively and actively by paraphrasing for accuracy
Shares ideas and resources	Rarely shares ideas or resources	Sometimes shares ideas or resources	Frequently shares ideas or resources	Routinely shares ideas and resources

Criteria	Rarely	Sometimes	Usually	Consistently
Willingly does his/her share of the work	Constant encouragement needed to work	Occasionally needs encouragement to work	Requires no encouragement to work	Works in a self-directed manner and encourages others
Uses group time wisely	Rarely stays on task or often distracts the group	Sometimes stays on task or distracts the group	Often stays on task and sometimes focuses group back on task	Always stays on task and directs group back on task
Adapts his/her role to the group's needs	Waits to be assigned a role in a group	Assumes certain roles independently	Often assumes different roles, including leadership	Routinely accepts different roles, including leadership, and helps with group organization

*Adapted from englishbulldogs.ca/grade10/pdf/Learning%20Skills%20Rubric.pdf

Appendix D

Gathering Evidence and Information

Minimum expectations for assessment:

External Assessments (sometimes referred to as Standardized Tests)

- Grade 2–9 students take the NWEA Map test twice a year in October and April.

- Grade 10–11 students take the PSAT test.

- Grade 12 students take the SAT test as many times as they wish during their senior year.

- IB candidates write the IB examinations in May.

Common Assessments

Teams and departments of all grades and subjects work together to develop common assessments.

- KG2–G7 teachers use common rubrics for On-Demand Units of Study Writing Workshop pieces.

- Grade 1–5 students are administered the Developmental Reading Assessment (DRA) twice per year (KG2 students take part in the second test as well).

Summative Assessments

- Each teacher must give students repeated opportunities to demonstrate their mastery of skills and content before each grading period.

Formative Assessments

- Formative assessments provide feedback for students to improve their learning and, as a result, perform better on summative assessments.

Self-Assessments

- Self-assessments are used in all grades/subjects in varying ways and frequency.

Works Cited

Betts, B. (2008). *Assessment for improving learning.* Cummaquid, MA: Teacher Training Center for International Educators.

Marzano, R. J. (2006). *Classroom assessment and grading that work.* Alexandria, VA: Association for Supervision and Curriculum Development.

New Zealand Ministry of Education. (2010, May). *The school curriculum: Design and review.* Accessed at http://nzcurriculum.tki. org.nz on May 15, 2015.

Tomlinson, C. A. (2008). The goals of differentiation. *Educational Leadership, 66*(3), 26–31.

Source: American International School Riyadh. (2014–2015). *AIS-R assessment, evaluation, and reporting practices and procedures 2014–15.* Accessed at https://docs.google.com/document/d/110eN0Fh0 gDG2P41WFM4h5MnjygGTzohHPYz2zbLvQL4/edit?usp=sharing on June 8, 2015.

REFERENCES AND RESOURCES

Ad Hoc Committee to Review Policies Regarding Assessment and Grading. (2014, August 5). *Report from the ad hoc committee to review policies regarding assessment and grading.* Princeton, NJ: Princeton University.

Ainsworth, L. (2003). *Power standards: Identifying the standards that matter the most.* Englewood, CO: Advanced Learning Press.

Ainsworth, L., & Christinson, J. (1998). *Student-generated rubrics: An assessment model to help all students succeed.* Orangeburg, NY: Seymour.

Alliance for Excellent Education. (2010, June 9). *The economic benefits of reducing the dropout rate in the nation's largest metropolitan areas.* Accessed at http://all4ed.org/reports-factsheets/the-economic-benefits -of-reducing-the-dropout-rate-in-the-nations-largest-metropolitan-areas on March 2, 2015.

American International School Riyadh. (2014–2015). *AIS-R assessment, evaluation, and reporting practices and procedures 2014–15.* Accessed at https://docs.google.com/document/d/110eN0Fh0gDG2P41WFM 4h5MnjygGTzohHPYz2zbLvQL4/edit?usp=sharing on June 8, 2015.

Amnesty International. (2008). *Amnesty International report 2008: The state of the world's human rights.* London: Author.

Appoquinimink School District. (2006). *Appoquinimink School District grading policy.* Accessed at www.cedarlaneschool.org/pdf/grading%20 policy.pdf on May 6, 2015.

Azar, B. (2010). Sink or skim? Tackle that endless pile of books and journal articles with the help of these reading tips. *GradPSYCH.* Accessed at www.apa.org/gradpsych/2010/11/skim.aspx on July 22, 2015.

Barnstable West Barnstable Elementary School. (2015). *Standard based report cards.* Accessed at www.barnstable.k12.ma.us/Page/505 on May 6, 2015.

Bidwell, A. (2014, August 20). Common Core support in free fall. *U.S. News and World Report*. Accessed at www.usnews.com/news/articles /2014/08/20/common-core-support-waning-most-now-oppose-standards -national-surveys-show on July 20, 2015.

Bracey, G. W. (2005). Tips for readers of research: How mean is the median? *Phi Delta Kappan, 87*(1), 92–93.

Brookhart, S. M. (2003). *Grading.* Upper Saddle River, NJ: Prentice Hall.

Calkins, L. M. (1983). *Lessons from a child: On the teaching and learning of writing.* Portsmouth, NH: Heinemann.

Calkins, L. M. (1994). *The art of teaching writing* (New ed.). Portsmouth, NH: Heinemann.

Campbell, D. T., & Stanley, J. C. (1963). *Experimental and quasi-experimental designs for research.* Chicago: Rand McNally.

City, E. A., Elmore, R. F., Fiarman, S. E., & Teitel, L. (2009). *Instructional rounds in education: A network approach to improving teaching and learning.* Cambridge, MA: Harvard Education Press.

Clymer, J. B., & Wiliam, D. (2007). Improving the way we grade science. *Educational Leadership, 64*(4), 36–42.

Colvin, G. (2008). *Talent is overrated: What really separates world-class performers from everybody else.* New York: Portfolio.

Committee on School Health. (2000). Corporal punishment in schools. *Pediatrics, 106*(2), 343.

Corbalan, M., Plaza, I., Hervas, E., A.-J. Zaragoza, E., & Arcega, F. (2013). Reduction of the students' evaluation of education quality questionnaire. *Proceedings of the 2013 Federated Conference on Computer Science and Information Systems*, 695–702. Accessed at https://fedcsis.org /proceedings/2013/pliks/29.pdf on July 16, 2015.

Dallas Independent School District. (n.d.). *PK–12 guidelines for grading.* Accessed at www.dallasisd.org/cms/lib/TX01001475/Centricity /Domain/172/documents/Grading%20Policy/gradingguidelines.pdf on May 6, 2015.

Darling-Hammond, L. (2010). *The flat world and education: How America's commitment to equity will determine our future.* New York: Teachers College Press.

Darling-Hammond, L., & Sykes, G. (Eds.). (1999). *Teaching as the learning profession: Handbook of policy and practice.* San Francisco: Jossey-Bass.

Deutschman, A. (2007). *Change or die: Could you change when change matters most?* New York: HarperCollins.

Duckworth, A. L., Peterson, C., Matthews, M. D., & Kelly, D. R. (2007). Grit: Perseverance and passion for long-term goals. *Journal of Personality and Social Psychology, 92*(6), 1087–1101.

DuFour, R., DuFour, R., & Eaker, R. (2008). *Revisiting professional learning communities at work: New insights for improving schools.* Bloomington, IN: Solution Tree Press.

DuFour, R., & Marzano, R. J. (2009). High-leverage strategies for principal leadership. *Educational Leadership, 66*(5), 62–68.

Dweck, C. S. (2006). *Mindset: The new psychology of success.* New York: Random House.

Elliott, S. (2013, December 19). *The basics of A to F grading in Indiana: Changes and controversy.* Accessed at http://in.chalkbeat.org/2013/12/19 /the-basics-of-a-to-f-grading-in-indiana-changes-and-controversy/# .VOXKzkK_SfR on February 19, 2015.

Ericsson, K. A., Charness, N., Hoffman, R. R., & Feltovich, P. J. (Eds.). (2006). *The Cambridge handbook of expertise and expert performance.* New York: Cambridge University Press.

Fairfax County Public Schools, Department of Accountability. (2008, December). *Fairfax County Public Schools (FCPS): An investigation of the grading policy.* Fairfax, VA: Author. Accessed at www.fairgrade.net/media /fairgrade/GradingPolicyInvestigationReport.pdf on July 22, 2015.

Fisher, R., & Ury, W. (2011). *Getting to yes: Negotiating agreement without giving in* (3rd ed.). New York: Penguin.

Fontana Unified School District. (2011). *Secondary grading policy.* Accessed at www.fusd.net/district/schsupport/secondary/grading%20policy.pdf on May 6, 2015.

Frederick County Public Schools. (n.d.). *High school secondary report card (grades 9–12).* Accessed at www.fcps.org/cms/lib02/MD01000577 /Centricity/Domain/28/examples/HS-reportcard.pdf on May 6, 2015.

Fullan, M. (2008a). *The six secrets of change: What the best leaders do to help their organizations survive and thrive.* San Francisco: Jossey-Bass.

Fullan, M. (2008b). *What's worth fighting for in the principalship* (2nd ed.). New York: Teachers College Press.

Fullan, M. (2010). *All systems go: The change imperative for whole system reform.* Thousand Oaks, CA: Corwin Press.

Fullan, M. (2011). *Change leader: Learning to do what matters most*. San Francisco: Jossey-Bass.

Fullan, M. (2013). *Stratosphere: Integrating technology, pedagogy, and change knowledge*. New York: Pearson.

Gallagher, W. (2009). *Rapt: Attention and the focused life*. New York: Penguin.

Gawande, A. (2009). *The checklist manifesto: How to get things right*. New York: Metropolitan Books.

Georgetown Independent School District. (2012). *Georgetown ISD 2011–12 grading guidelines*. Accessed at http://web.georgetownisd.org/filing_cabinet/curriculum/GradingRegulations.pdf on May 6, 2015.

Gladwell, M. (2008). *Outliers: The story of success*. New York: Little, Brown.

Gladwell, M. (2009). *What the dog saw and other adventures*. New York: Little, Brown.

Great Schools Partnership. (2013, August 20). *The glossary of education reform: Power standards*. Accessed at http://edglossary.org/power-standards/ on July 16, 2015.

Guskey, T. R. (2000). Grading policies that work against standards . . . and how to fix them. *NASSP Bulletin, 84*(620), 20–29.

Guskey, T. R. (2002). *How's my kid doing? A parent's guide to grades, marks, and report cards*. San Francisco: Jossey-Bass.

Guskey, T. R. (Ed.). (2009). *The teacher as assessment leader*. Bloomington, IN: Solution Tree Press.

Guskey, T. R. (2015). *On your mark: Challenging the conventions of grading and reporting*. Bloomington, IN: Solution Tree Press.

Guskey, T. R., & Bailey, J. M. (2001). *Developing grading and reporting systems for student learning*. Thousand Oaks, CA: Corwin Press.

Harlem Village Academies. (2015). *Data and facts*. Accessed at http://harlemvillageacademies.org/data-and-facts/ on July 16, 2015.

Hattie, J. (2009). *Visible learning: A synthesis of over 800 meta-analyses relating to achievement*. New York: Routledge.

Hattie, J. (2012). *Visible learning for teachers: Maximizing impact on learning*. New York: Routledge.

Hattie, J., & Yates, G. (2014). *Visible learning and the science of how we learn*. New York: Routledge.

Haycock, K., & Crawford, C. (2008, April). Closing the teacher quality gap. *Educational Leadership, 65*(7), 14–19.

Heath, C., & Heath, D. (2010). *Switch: How to change things when change is hard.* New York: Broadway Books.

Hensley, D., & Carlin, D. (2005). *Mastering competitive debate* (7th ed.). Logan, IA: Perfection Learning.

Herrnstein, R. J., & Murray, C. (1994). *The bell curve: Intelligence and class structure in American life.* New York: Free Press.

Human Rights Watch. (2008). *A violent education: Corporal punishment of children in U.S. public schools.* New York: Author. Accessed at www.aclu .org/pdfs/humanrights/aviolenteducation_report.pdf on February 26, 2010.

Ingersoll, R., & Perda, D. (2009). *How high is teacher turnover and is it a problem?* Philadelphia: Consortium for Policy Research in Education, University of Pennsylvania.

International Society for Technology in Education. (2015). *Global reach of the ISTE Standards.* Accessed at www.iste.org/standards/standards-in -action/global-reach on July 16, 2015.

Kafer, K. (2005, March 1). U.S. girl students outperform boys in most subjects, study finds. *Heartland.* Accessed at www.heartland.org/policybot /results/16492/US_Girl_Students_Outperform_Boys_in_Most_Subjects _Study_Finds.html on June 10, 2010.

Kim, W. C., & Mauborgne, R. (2003, January). Fair process: Managing in the knowledge economy. *Harvard Business Review.* Accessed at https:// hbr.org/2003/01/fair-process-managing-in-the-knowledge-economy on March 2, 2015.

Kohn, A. (1999). *Punished by rewards: The trouble with gold stars, incentive plans, A's, praise, and other bribes.* New York: Houghton Mifflin.

Kotter, J. P. (1996). *Leading change.* Boston: Harvard Business School Press.

Kotter, J. P. (2008). *A sense of urgency.* Boston: Harvard Business School Press.

Lehrer, J. (2009). *How we decide.* New York: Houghton Mifflin.

Lemov, D. (2010). *Teach like a champion: 49 techniques that put students on the path to college, grades K–12.* San Francisco: Jossey-Bass.

Lexington Public Schools. (n.d.a). *Lexington Public Schools elementary report card* [grade 05]. Accessed at http://lps.lexingtonma.org/cms/lib2 /MA01001631/Centricity/Domain/842/LPSGr5SBRC11sep14.pdf on May 6, 2015.

Lexington Public Schools. (n.d.b). *Lexington Public Schools elementary report card* [grade KF]. Accessed at http://lps.lexingtonma.org/cms /lib2/MA01001631/Centricity/Domain/842/KSBRC07nov132.pdf on May 6, 2015.

Linn, R. L. (1998, November). *Assessments and accountability: CSE technical report 490.* Los Angeles: Center for the Study of Evaluation.

Marsh, H. W. (1984). Students' evaluations of university teaching: Dimensionality, reliability, validity, potential biases, and utility. *Journal of Educational Psychology, 76*(5), 707–754.

Marshall, K. (2009). *Rethinking teacher supervision and evaluation: How to work smart, build collaboration, and close the achievement gap.* San Francisco: Jossey-Bass.

Marzano, R. J. (2007). *The art and science of teaching: A comprehensive framework for effective instruction.* Alexandria, VA: Association for Supervision and Curriculum Development.

Marzano, R. J. (2009). *Designing and teaching learning goals and objectives.* Bloomington, IN: Marzano Research.

Marzano, R. J. (2010). *Formative assessment and standards-based grading.* Bloomington, IN: Marzano Research.

Marzano, R. J., & Kendall, J. S. (1998). *Implementing standards-based education.* Washington, DC: National Education Association.

McAfee, A. (2009, November 20). It's time to embrace evidence-based medicine. *Harvard Business Review.* Accessed at https://hbr.org/2009/11 /its-time-to-embrace-evidenceba on March 3, 2015.

McTighe, J., & Wiggins, G. (2013). *Essential questions: Opening doors to student understanding.* Alexandra, VA: Association for Supervision and Curriculum Development.

Mester, M. (2011). *The effects of writer's workshop on writing achievement in the kindergarten classroom* (Doctoral dissertation). Walden University, Minneapolis, MN.

National Constitution Center. (2015). *Amendment X: Rights reserved to states or people.* Accessed at http://constitutioncenter.org/constitution /the-amendments/amendment-10-powers-of-the-states-and-people on July 20, 2015.

National Governors Association Center for Best Practices & Council of Chief State School Officers. (2010a). *Common Core State Standards for English language arts and literacy in history/social studies, science, and technical subjects*. Washington, DC: Authors. Accessed at www.corestandards.org /assets/CCSSI_ELA%20Standards.pdf on April 30, 2015.

National Governors Association Center for Best Practices & Council of Chief State School Officers. (n.d.). *Common Core State Standards for English and language arts & literacy in history/social studies, science, and technical subjects: Appendix C—Samples of student writing.* Accessed at www.corestandards.org/assets/Appendix_C.pdf on July 16, 2015.

National Governors Association Center for Best Practices & Council of Chief State School Officers. (2010b). *Common Core State Standards for mathematics.* Washington, DC: Authors. Accessed at www.corestandards.org/assets/CCSSI_Math%20Standards.pdf on April 30, 2015.

Oak Middle School. (n.d.). *Shrewsbury Public Schools grade 8 report card.* Accessed at http://schools.shrewsbury-ma.gov/egov/docs/1262891914 _266906.pdf on May 6, 2015.

O'Connor, K. (2009). *How to grade for learning, K–12* (3rd ed.). Thousand Oaks, CA: Corwin Press.

O'Connor, K. (2011). *A repair kit for grading: 15 fixes for broken grades* (2nd ed.). Boston: Pearson.

Ohanian, S. (1999). *One size fits few: The folly of educational standards.* Portsmouth, NH: Heinemann Press.

Patterson, K., Grenny, J., Maxfield, D., McMillan, R., & Switzler, A. (2008). *Influencer: The power to change anything.* New York: McGraw-Hill.

Pérez-Peña, R. (2012, September 7). Studies find more students cheating, with high achievers no exception. *The New York Times.* Accessed at www.nytimes.com/2012/09/08/education/studies-show-more -students-cheat-even-high-achievers.html?_r=0 on July 16, 2015.

Pfeffer, J., & Sutton, R. I. (2006a). Evidence-based management. *Harvard Business Review, 84*(1), 62–74.

Pfeffer, J., & Sutton, R. I. (2006b). *Hard facts, dangerous half-truths, and total nonsense: Profiting from evidence-based management.* Boston: Harvard Business School Press.

Pink, D. H. (2009). *Drive: The surprising truth about what motivates us.* New York: Riverhead Books.

Pogrow, S. (2009). *Teaching content outrageously: How to captivate all students and accelerate learning, grades 4–12.* San Francisco: Jossey-Bass.

Popham, W. J. (2008). *Transformative assessment.* Alexandria, VA: Association for Supervision and Curriculum Development.

Porter, J. M., & Jelinek, D. (2011). Evaluating inter-rater reliability of a national assessment model for teacher performance. *International Journal of Educational Policies, 5*(2), 74–87.

Putnam, R. (2015). *Our kids: The American dream in crisis.* New York: Simon & Schuster.

Reeves, D. B. (2004). *Accountability for learning: How teachers and school leaders can take charge.* Alexandria, VA: Association for Supervision and Curriculum Development.

Reeves, D. B. (2006a). *The learning leader: How to focus school improvement for better results.* Alexandria, VA: Association for Supervision and Curriculum Development.

Reeves, D. B. (2006b). Preventing 1,000 failures. *Educational Leadership, 64*(3), 88–89.

Reeves, D. B. (2008a). Effective grading practices. *Educational Leadership, 65*(5), 85–87.

Reeves, D. B. (2008b). *Reframing teacher leadership to improve your school.* Alexandria, VA: Association for Supervision and Curriculum Development.

Reeves, D. B. (2009a). *Assessing educational leaders: Evaluating performance for improved individual and organizational results* (2nd ed.). Thousand Oaks, CA: Corwin Press.

Reeves, D. B. (2009b). *Leading change in your school: How to conquer myths, build commitment, and get results.* Alexandria, VA: Association for Supervision and Curriculum Development.

Reeves, D. B. (2009c, September 14). Remaking the grade, from A to D. *The Chronicle of Higher Education.* Accessed at http://chronicle.com /article/Remaking-the-Grade-From-A-to/48352 on March 15, 2010.

Reeves, D. B. (2011a). *Finding your leadership focus: What matters most for student results.* New York: Teachers College Press.

Reeves, D. B. (2011b). Skeptics and cynics. *American School Board Journal, 198*(10), 40–41.

Reeves, D. B. (2012a, June). Uninformative assessment. *American School Board Journal, 199*(6), 34.

Reeves, D. B. (2012b, July). The ketchup solution. *American School Board Journal, 199*(7), 35–36.

Rosenthal, R., & DiMatteo, M. R. (2001). Meta-analysis: Recent developments in quantitative methods for literature reviews. *Annual Review of Psychology, 52*, 59–82.

Roueche, J. E., Roueche, S. D., & Ely, E. (2002, November). A centralized approach to developmental education: A collegewide strategy for student success. *Southern Association of Community, Junior, and Technical Colleges Newsletter, 37*(1), 5–16.

Salem, A. A. M. S. (2013, June 3). The effect of using writer's workshop approach on developing basic writing skills (mechanics of writing) of prospective teachers of English in Egypt. *English Language Teaching, 6*(7), 33–45.

Sanders, W. L. (1998). Value-added assessment. *The School Administrator, 55*(11). Accessed at www.aasa.org/SchoolAdministratorArticle.aspx?id=15066 on March 2, 2015.

Schmoker, M. (2005). No turning back: The ironclad case for professional learning communities. In R. DuFour, R. Eaker, & R. DuFour (Eds.), *On common ground: The power of professional learning communities* (pp. 135–153). Bloomington, IN: Solution Tree Press.

Schmoker, M. (2006). *Results now: How we can achieve unprecedented improvements in teaching and learning.* Alexandria, VA: Association for Supervision and Curriculum Development.

Springfield Public Schools. (2010). *District grading framework.* Accessed at www.sps.springfield.ma.us/webContent/Policies/SPS%20Grading%20Framework.pdf on May 6, 2015.

Stein, N. (2000, October 2). The world's most admired companies. *Fortune.* Accessed at http://archive.fortune.com/magazines/fortune/fortune_archive/2000/10/02/288448/index.htm on July 16, 2015.

Steinhauer, J., & Rich, M. (2015, July 8). Lawmakers move to limit government's role in education. *The New York Times.* Accessed at www.nytimes.com/2015/07/09/us/lawmakers-move-to-limit-governments-role-in-education.html on July 15, 2015.

Stober, D. R., & Grant, A. M. (Eds.). (2006). *Evidenced-based coaching handbook: Putting best practices to work for your clients.* Hoboken, NJ: Wiley.

Strauss, V. (2014, September 18). Nineteen states still allow corporal punishment in school. *The Washington Post.* Accessed at www.washingtonpost.com/blogs/answer-sheet/wp/2014/09/18/19-states-still-allow-corporal-punishment-in-school)/ on July 21, 2015.

Tomahawk School. (2013). *Student progress report.* Accessed at www.psd70
.ab.ca/documents/Sample_Grade_7_Report_Card.pdf on May 6, 2015.

U.S. News and World Report. (2015). *Harlem Village Academy Charter
School Ehvacs: Student body.* Accessed at www.usnews.com/education
/best-high-schools/new-york/districts/new-york-city-public-schools
/harlem-village-academy-charter-school-ehvacs-92131/student-body
on July 16, 2015.

Wiggins, G. (1998). *Educative assessment: Designing assessments to inform
and improve student performance.* San Francisco: Jossey-Bass.

Willingham, D. T. (2009). *Why don't students like school? A cognitive scientist answers questions about how the mind works and what it means for
the classroom.* San Francisco: Jossey-Bass.

Zhao, Y. (2014). *Who's afraid of the big bad dragon? Why China has the best
(and worst) education system in the world.* San Francisco: Jossey-Bass.

Zwaagstra, M. (2012, August 30). *No-zero grading policies in schools not supported by the evidence.* Accessed at www.troymedia.com/2012/08/30
/no-zero-grading-policies-in-schools-not-supported-by-the-evidence on
February 11, 2015.

INDEX

On Your Mark

By Thomas R. Guskey

Create and sustain a learning environment where students thrive and stakeholders are accurately informed of student progress. Clarify the purpose of grades, craft a vision statement aligned with this purpose, and discover research-based strategies to implement effective grading and reporting practices.

BKF606

Inspiring Creativity and Innovation in K–12

By Douglas Reeves

Encourage a culture of innovation and creativity. Explore the four essentials for developing a creative, mistake-tolerant culture; investigate teaching and leadership beliefs and practices that undermine creativity; and discover strategies for successfully navigating challenges that your team may face along the way.

BKF664

Redefining Fair

By Damian Cooper
Foreword by Michael Fullan

Learn how to define proficiency accurately and differentiate to help all students achieve it. Using stories, strategies, case histories, and sample documents, the author explains how to implement equitable instruction, assessment, grading, and reporting practices for diverse 21st century learners.

BKF412

Ahead of the Curve

Edited by Douglas Reeves
By Larry Ainsworth, Lisa Almeida, Anne Davies, Richard DuFour, Linda Gregg, Thomas R. Guskey, Robert J. Marzano, Ken O'Connor, Douglas Reeves, Rick Stiggins, Stephen White, and Dylan Wiliam

Leaders in education contribute their perspectives on effective assessment design and implementation, sending out a call for redirecting assessment to improve student achievement and inform instruction.

BKF232

"Excellent engagement
in what truly matters
in **assessment**.

Great examples!"

—Carol Johnson, superintendent,
Central Dauphin School District, Pennsylvania

 PD Services

Our experts draw from decades of research and their own experiences to bring you
practical strategies for designing and implementing quality assessments. You can choose
from a range of customizable services, from a one-day overview to a multiyear process.

Book your assessment PD today!
888.763.9045

Solution Tree